Parents In Crisis

By
Jim Binney, D.Min

The Counselor's Pen Publications
Greenville, SC

Requests for information should be addressed to:
The Counselor's Pen
P.O. Box 25444
Greenville, SC 29616
http://www.leadministries.net

Table of Contents

DEDICATION

Dedicated with love to my son Jonathan Kyle Binney, who, as his name implies, is a "gift from God" to his mom and dad. Because of him and the paths we have trod together over the years, we have learned much of love and of God. We love you, son.

WITH SPECIAL THANKS

To Attorney John Blume and his staff and the team at The Death Penalty Project of the Cornell Law School who have unselfishly devoted themselves to our son and our family.

PREFACE

Never before in recorded history has the family been under attack as it is today! The "war against the family" is in progress, and a primary battle ground in the parent-child relationship; *"...in the last days perilous times shall come;...for men shall be disobedient to parents" (2 Timothy 3:1-2)*. The world, the flesh, and the devil are outdoing themselves in raining havoc and destruction on the home and the target of choice is the children.

The world targets them through its widespread influence through the applications of modern technologies. From T.V. to computers, from hand held electronic games to text messaging, young minds are absorbed and focused on mind-numbing distractions which insure that they rarely have time or energy to focus on the things of God.

Even more serious than distractions to worldliness are temptations to sinfulness. A principal of a Christian high school recently informed me that the most serious problem they're currently facing is the student practice of texting pornographic images to one another.

The flesh is a co-conspirator with the world in this bombardment of youth. It is, after all, a natural response for undisciplined minds and hearts to be drawn away by out-of-control desires.

The devil is not to be overlooked in this struggle. He has targeted the young with every weapon at his disposal with shocking results. In a survey of 2,000 Christian school students, it was found that many had experienced an encounter with the supernatural. Fifty per cent of junior high kids and 47% of senior high reported they had seen a presence in their room. When asked if they had ever heard voices in their subconscious minds, "yes" was the response of 57% of junior high students and 70% of senior high!

Christian parents who are entrusted with the protection of their children are left to wonder how they can possibly fulfill their mandate. Caught ill-prepared by their child's advanced knowledge of technology, and burdened with a heavy weight of responsibility, they are also crippled by an abysmal lack of training or knowledge in exactly how to do their job. No schools exist to train young parents on how to shape and mold a child's mind. Rare is the teaching on how to help the parent of an adolescent work through his rebellion and grow in his walk with God. Few resources are available to the parents of adult children who long to re-build bridges with their estranged offspring. Instead, parents are left to fend for themselves in a desperate on the job training where learning is largely by trial and error.

On the other hand, help for the parent of the newborn seems to be readily available; books, classes, seminars, and DVDs abound on how to produce the perfect child.

Enthusiastic and rabid teachers and even pastors promote the teachings of determinism; a belief which insists that a person's character, decisions, and even their ultimate destiny is determined by outside influences, namely parenting. Heavy on promise and strong in methodology, they promote the guarantee of certain success if their teachings are embraced, and warn of failure if they're not.

Foundational to these teachings is an underlying assumption that not only can any parent shape the soul of a child into a shining trophy but that every parent is responsible to do so. No failure is tolerated by these purveyors of perfection, and there is plenty of blame to heap on unwary parents who fail to produce.

Parents by the thousands enter parenthood with high hopes and a strong sense of calling. They know their responsibility is heavy; but buoyed with the promise of ultimate success, they blindly forge ahead with high expectations.

But the higher the expectation, the greater the disappointment when not realized. *"Hope deferred maketh the heart sick" (Proverbs 13:12),* and surely there are many heart-sick parents found in the wake of unfulfilled desires and broken dreams.

When the infant becomes a toddler and enters the "terrible twos", the first hint of frustration emerges. As they grow into the junior years, it grows larger; but when the teen years have peaked, the frustration is often replaced by a sense of betrayal. What happened to the promises they had been taught? Where was their trophy child?

Then comes the guilt. All too quickly and glibly the criticisms begin, slowly at first, but increasing in volume and intensity as the child gets older. These are not just from friends and relatives but, more painfully, from the parents' own hearts. If what they have been taught is true, it is their fault that this child is so rebellious. The floodwaters of despair rise to critical mass in their souls. They find themselves drowning with little to support them. They long for someone to understand. They strain to hear a voice of hope, but instead, they are met with a chorus of voices bent on reminding them of their failure.

Thus the purpose of this book; it is meant to offer real biblical instruction for the struggling parent. Here will be found a strong undergirding of scriptural principles upon which are built practical methods of Christian parenting.

The discouraged parent will find words of hope in this volume. At the same time, you will be faced with the reality of parental sin or failure if it exists, and exhortations to make them right. However, because the scale of parental teachings lean so heavily to the side of blaming parents and excusing children, in the interest of parity, the general tone of this book will be more inclined toward encouragement than condemnation of the parent.

Some of the chapters have been published in various Christian periodicals and others written expressly for this book. Because of these multiple sources, the reader is asked to bear with the author if some material overlaps.

Chapter one is a frank admission by the author of his own struggles as a parent. He addresses the needs of parents from a heart of compassion because he's been there.

Chapter two addresses common but dangerous assumptions about a child's true salvation. It is foolish to treat a natural man like a spiritual one, and yet the basis of many professions of salvation is very shaky indeed! This chapter will help you in evaluating the true state of your child's soul.

Chapter three challenges an all-too-common problem in parenting, a lack of goals. This chapter provides some very specific biblical goals for parents for every Christian parent.

Chapter four features an emphasis on balance in the pursuit of Christian parenting. Imbalance spells the death knell of many high aspirations.

Chapter five provides practical steps of discipline to use in taking the child from the offense to the correction based on biblical principles and workable methods.

Chapter six outlines a method of scriptural praying for you to use for your child. Praying is one thing; targeted praying another, and scripturally targeted prayers quite another!

Chapter seven confronts the age-old problem of gospel hardening. Protecting Christian school kids from this common malady is a challenge to the best parent. You will find help here.

Chapters eight through eleven take on the giant of determinism. Who really is responsible for the child's decisions? Rightly interpreting the Bible around some fuzzy teaching on this subject, this chapter offers a needed focus.

The section of appendices holds a wealth of supportive information for a variety of needs, and is almost a book in itself. There is help for parents of "A.D.D." children, and adopted children. There is needed guidance in interpreting labels of one "disorder" or another assigned to your child. You will find a clear biblical plan for helping your child experience lasting change, and answers for important questions about pastors and their children as well.

The end result is that you hold in your hands an unusual volume; a book which addresses the unique challenges of the parent of the wayward child. It is our hope that you will find more answers than questions, but in the event that you may have some questions, we invite your response. Feel free to contact us. Help us to improve our ministry to you.

We would love to hear testimonies of hope and victory to share with our readers. If you care to write your story, it will be gratefully received.

Be assured of our prayers for you as you read.

The Publisher

Chapter One

A Crisis of My Own

"Hope deferred maketh the heart sick" - *Proverbs 13:12*

Expectations can be the best of servants or the worst of masters. And when it comes to marriage and children, runaway expectations based on little but wishful thinking can be a downright tyrant! When they are not based squarely on the Word of God and the will of God, they literally set up the unwary for disappointment. Proverbs 13:12 makes this abundantly clear. When a hope (expectation) is deferred i.e. postponed or even terminated, the heart gets "sick" or discouraged and even depressed.

But when the expectation is of God, originating with Him and communicated to us by Him, the soul finds stability. King David was confident that he would not be "greatly moved" because of this very principle; *"My soul, wait thou only upon God; for my expectation is from him"*. *(Psalm 62:5)*.

Marriages and families that begin with man-made expectations are doomed to disappointment, but this is precisely how most families begin. They are based on an abundance of worldly ideals and romantic notions and give

1

little attention to God's design. Parental approaches to child rearing are formed in the same way.

In our marriage, for example, we had a double let-down because of two major misplaced expectations; first, we expected to have children like everyone else, and second, we expected that if we trained those children rightly, they would turn out to be poster children for Christianity.

We Expected to have Children

I have always had a soft spot for little children. Sandra has told me that she can tell when children are around just by looking at my face. An unavoidable smile comes over me when I see them. Nothing is cuter than little children (at least when they are on good behavior). While a pastor in Michigan and later in North Carolina, I loved to listen to the laughter and giggles and excited voices of children on the church's school playground. I could not resist joining in despite my attire of street clothes. (I ruined more than one pair of dress shoes playing soccer).

If children are my soft spot, little girls are my Achilles heel. I love little boys but I adore little girls. They seem so demure and innocent and incapable of wrongdoing. A big regret of mine is that I never had a daughter and could never understand why God did not give me one. It might have something to do with the fact that I cannot envision a little girl needing a spanking. Look at those little angelic faces! Study them while they are asleep…the epitome of innocence. I am amazed at the "abusive" parents who actually see sin instead of innocence and even (gasp!) spank them. (Please indulge me on this point, and don't write me telling me of the true nature of little girls. You might destroy another dream of mine.)

Like many newly married couples, Sandra and I nourished dreams of a little family complete with beautiful and well-behaved children. We hoped for a boy and girl at the very least, and more if God so willed. But, as time passed and no children were forthcoming, we began to get concerned. We went to the doctor, had tests, followed the doctor's advice, kept charts, etc., but still nothing.

After eight long years of disappointment, we began considering adoption. After all, the child's heritage notwithstanding, we would be his parents and he our own child. His little heart would be a blank slate on which we would write his destiny. We believed Proverbs 22:6 fervently; *Train up a child in the way he should go: and when he is old, he will not depart from it."* In other words, with right training, we <u>could</u> create the poster child for Christianity! It made no difference if the child was our birth child or our adopted child. We believed that this verse was a promise to take to the bank!

The disappointment of our barrenness was finally to be overcome by the hopefulness of adoption. We sincerely believed this to be God's provision for our emptiness, and so, we set out on the journey that only adoptive parents can understand. We searched and researched, applied and reapplied, and finally found a place that would help us. Our expectations would soon be disappointed once again, however, and our faith sorely tested. Our efforts were in vain; not once, nor twice, but three times! On each occasion we had a child within our grasp only to have one of the parents change their mind for one reason or another. We had almost given up hope when our pastor, Dr. Jack Hyles, stepped in and began to work on our behalf.

Through Evangelist Lester Roloff, who had a home for unwed mothers in Mississippi, we found a sixteen year old girl who had gotten pregnant and was ready to deliver. We rushed to the hospital and carried home a six and a half pound baby boy! We knew nothing of the child's family heritage, even his mother's name. But we didn't care! After all, none of those things mattered! We could overcome all difficulties with the right training. And besides, this baby was the spitting image of his parents. In short order, we began to hear comments like, "Well, you can sure tell whose child this is"!

We Expected to Rear a Poster Child for Christianity

And so we set out on a journey of hope, hope which had transcended all the disappointments of the past, hope in the promise of Proverbs 22:6, hope in the certainty of rearing a model Christian young man, hope of the joy and pride of watching this child grow up to honor his parents and glorify his God. And to our delight, this hope loomed large over us. We saw things in this boy that gave our hope an even greater boost; his tender spirit, obedient will, and loving heart was a source of constant delight. He would tell the truth to his own detriment, shunning a lie as if not even a consideration. He mimicked me as a miniature preacher with a makeshift pulpit in the living room. He would lead singing and then preach a sermon to anyone who would listen. As he grew older, we heard reports of amazed neighbors and store owners who marveled at his Bible knowledge and boldness in witnessing. His innate musical talent found fertile soil in his violin and piano lessons, even resulting in his accompanying special music before he had formal lessons and could read music. (Let's face it; the boy was a genius!)

Then came the sixth grade year of school when we moved from the home of his birth. He began to act out in school, hang out with the tough boys, and soon reports began coming to us of his misbehavior; little things at first but they quickly became more significant, and then shocking! His school work suffered during this time and we tried to get him special tutoring. We learned that he was not a visual learner and struggled with classroom lecture-type teaching. He was soon diagnosed with A.D.D., and as he felt less and less accepted by the good kids, he gravitated to the baser element. He began a pattern of running away from home, stealing, and getting in trouble with the law. When he would run away, he would write us the sweetest notes explaining this wasn't our fault, that he loved us, but somehow just had to do this. He would disappear for weeks or months at a time with us having little if any contact, wondering if he was okay or even alive. He was always demonstrative in his affection, enjoying a good hug and always ready to give one.

After another move and another bad track record at school, he went too far and began his checkered history of incarcerations. Over the next few years, we joined him for an agonizing journey from courtrooms to jails, and back to courtrooms and eventually state prisons beginning at age 16. We will never forget the first time we visited Jonathan in prison. We traveled to the New York State Prison at Albany, an imposing structure with ugly rust colored walls and filled with hardened criminals. As we awaited his arrival from his cell, we saw him; clothed in a prison issued jump suit and bound by dangling leg and arm irons which issued a discordant sound as they jingled and clanged around his body. Our hearts sank as we saw this frail wisp of a boy in this bastion of evil and perversion.

We had visited him in city and county jails before, still clinging to the hope that this prodigal would be jarred from his waywardness by the pig pen in which he found himself. But now, in this place, surrounded by despairing, hopeless men, I felt the hope drain from my body like air escaping out of a punctured tire. The agony of sorrow was so pervasive, so far reaching, so palpably evident in every fiber of my being, that my heart despaired and all my dreams came crashing down.

Not only did we not have our poster child, we didn't even have an average one. Despite our best efforts; our prayers, our teaching, multiple hours in church and Sunday

School, the best of teachers and youth workers, Christian camps, constant exposure to the cream of Christian leaders who visited our church and home – despite all this, he was now a common criminal.

And what of Proverbs 22:6? If it were true that a child's training determined his destiny, then one of two things were true: either I had failed as a parent, or God had lied to me. If it's true that one can reason from the training to the outcome, one can also reason from the outcome to the training. If good training begets good kids, bad kids are traceable to bad training; therefore, it was my fault. And if my son's failure was my fault, as a pastor and Christian leader, I had some serious issues to consider. If I had a wayward child, then according to the beliefs of many, I was not qualified to be a spiritual leader. This fear had become a companion of mine early on in Jonathan's departure from godliness and had only increased in its accusations as time progressed.

I knew there were people blaming me for his behavior, even people in the churches I pastored. After all, I had taught them to believe this way. And now it had come back to haunt me. I found myself questioning my right to minister. Was I unfit? Had I disqualified myself? Wasn't one of the chief qualifiers of the minister to be *"One that ruleth well his own house, having his children in subjection with all gravity" (1 Timothy 3:4)*? The accuser of the brethren had a great ally in me. Whatever efforts he made to derail my ministry needed little help. I was doing very well by myself. I berated myself while questioning my worth, my calling, my usefulness to God, and ultimately and shamefully, questioning God and His Word at the same time.

And through all this the heavens were made of brass; nothing I prayed, no matter how agonizing, seemed to be heard. The silence of God was deafening. His presence was nowhere to be found. I felt He had abandoned me to swing in the wind on the end of an inescapable rope. My friends were questioning me, the devil accusing me, hope eluding me, and even my God, it seemed, was failing me. I found myself swirling downward in a deepening whirlpool of blacker and darker despondency. There was nothing to which to cling, no one to whom to turn. Every expectation had come crashing down and the emptiness of my soul threatened to overwhelm me.

All these feelings were intensified by the common but misguided notion of those in ministry, that the pastorate was my very identity. It signified who I was and what I was. To have that taken from me was a form of spiritual neutering I could not endure. Now that I was disqualified, who was I? What was to become of me? What was I to do? There were no answers, only questions. A sense of hopelessness replaced my hope, despair robbed me of joy, the presence of Satan displaced any sense of God, and the thing I lived for, breathed for and thought at one point that I was willing to die for – the ministry – was being taken from me!

And I was not alone in my suffering; my dear wife Sandra had her own burdens to bear in all this. Because she was joined to me at the hip, and shared in everything I was and did, she had to travel through this valley of the shadow of death with me. There was even a point, to my shame, that I questioned her role as a mother. Unwilling to fully accept that I was to blame, I opted for a "flesh and blood" mentality and blamed her by default. If a child's misbehavior was traceable to bad parenting, and I felt that I was a good father, that left but one option.

But I was a drowning man grasping at straws; any straw of blame-shifting, denial, self-justification would do nicely if I could just find one. Like many parents, I blamed the church, the school, body chemicals, mental disorders, birthparents, society, the media, the culture…..give me something or someone to blame and I would grasp for them.

Through all this, God was at work. He never left me nor forsook me. He was shaping a vessel and molding a man. He was taking me to my extremity so He could comfort me in His love. He was identifying the idols of my heart that blocked my view of Him, targeting them, and lovingly knocking them over so I could see Him clearly. And He was also, and for this I am ever thankful to Him, directing my thinking to the one place of joy and hope and peace, the Word of God.

It began when I read a book on prodigals and the author referenced Ezekiel chapter 18. When I began to study this wonderful portion of Scripture, my eyes were opened. A blessed light began to penetrate the midnight darkness of my soul. The black cloud of despair which had been my constant companion began to lift to reveal the sunshine of truth. And the truth I saw amazed me! I realized that all this misery was of my own making. Because I had carelessly embraced the teachings of man and had never been fully persuaded in my own mind, I had flippantly embraced expectations and beliefs which had to be reexamined for my very sanity!

I confess to you that I began my search in the scriptures to find some truth, any morsel of truth which might comfort my beleaguered soul. For my marriage, my ministry, my future, and my very life, I needed hope! I determined to go to the Bible as my sole authority. I would not look to what man said the Bible taught, but I would dig it out for myself. I realized that I had been lazy in this regard, allowing well-meaning but misguided men to teach me what they, too, had been taught. Instead of searching the scriptures to see whether these things were so, and instead of being fully persuaded in my own mind, I had naively accepted as fact what another man said. I desperately needed to find out what God had said.

Lest someone might accuse me of merely seeking some relief from my pain, let me set your minds at ease…of course I did! Where else is one to go but to God? How do we learn of His mind apart from His Word? It is this very journey that is the basis of this book. I am comforting you with the comfort that God has been pleased to give me. *"Blessed be… the God of all comfort; Who comforteth us in all our tribulation, that we may be able to comfort them which are in any trouble, by the comfort wherewith we ourselves are comforted of God." (2 Cor. 1:3-4).* It was because of my trouble that I sought comfort from God, and it is that comfort which I now share with you, dear reader.

This book is not for everybody. It is meant for parents in crisis, those who desperately need some hope and comfort. Had someone given me this book twenty-five years ago, I probably would have rejected it out of hand. I still clung to the dream of the poster child and the belief that I could create him with my parenting. If that describes you, I bid you no evil. I pray for you. I ask for the same consideration. And should you honestly disagree with the findings of this book, feel free to express that disagreement, but with two conditions; first, that you clarify my views with me clearly before you represent me to others, and second, that if you have a disagreement, give me a biblical reason for it. If I can be shown that I was wrong from the Bible, I will retract what I have written. When someone comes to me with a sweet spirit and an open Bible, I can do no less. But don't come to me with traditions violated, man-made teachings ignored, or prideful assumptions threatened, as these are not reasons for disagreement. But if, after you have studied the evidence and weighed the scriptures and then find something amiss, I will gladly welcome your correction.

I found the hope I longed for. I regained the joy I had lost. I discovered a new commitment to ministry that had languished on the rocks of despair. And just in time. Hardly had I found firm biblical footing for my life, that a new storm hit me with hurricane force. I remember it like it was just yesterday; I was standing on a courthouse lawn awaiting my son's latest sentencing from a judge when I received a call on my cell phone that my mother was dying and expected to live only a few more days. Then I went into the courthouse and heard the death sentence pronounced upon my only child. As I write this, he languishes on death row in South Carolina awaiting the inevitable unless God intervenes through the appeal process.

But unlike in past times, when lesser announcements sent me into despair, like the psalmist, I was not greatly moved. I was jarred, of course, hurt beyond measure, and grieved for my son and my dear wife, but my heart was fixed and my feet planted on the solid ground of God's Word.

I thank God for this painful roller coaster ride with my son. It has never been boring but ever challenging, and it has also taught me things which no classroom or textbook could have done.

My ministry has been expanded by God exponentially through all this. Doors of ministry opportunity have been opened beyond my fondest hope. After all, few parents whose child told a lie or stole a candy bar from a convenience store think twice about confiding in someone whose son in on death row. They know they will not find a critic in me but hopefully someone to understand.

I don't know what pain you carry. I can't fully understand your pilgrimage as you read these words. The very fact that you are reading this may indicate a deep need for comfort and hope in your own heart or home. I can offer you only limited help, but I know Someone who understands fully and stands ready to minister amazing and abundant grace to you and your loved ones. He is touched with the feeling of your infirmities and that of your children. He holds their hearts in His hand and can turn them like the rivers of water.

I pray that you will find the hope that Sandra and I have found. May the following pages be used of our loving Lord to that end.

Chapter Two

Is Your Child Really a Christian?

"Examine yourselves, whether ye be in the faith…"
2 Corinthians 13:5

One of the greatest challenges facing a biblical counselor is trying to help a counselee who is not really a Christian. The source of the challenge is the biblical presumption that an unsaved person, called a "natural man" in the Bible, cannot understand spiritual things (1 Corinthians 2:14-16). He must first be saved from his sin, and then he will have spiritual discernment given by the Holy Spirit of God.

I once met a man who was struggling with some major disorders. He was plagued by them so severely that he was not able to function in normal society. He could no longer hold a job or go out in public. He had spent in excess of $30,000 in therapy and medications to overcome it, but all to no avail. The counseling seemed to get nowhere. He seemed incapable of absorbing the truth let alone living it. I had been counseling him as a Christian; and yet as I listened to him, he showed none of the evidences of salvation. I asked him, "Are you a born again Christian?" "Yes," he replied. "Tell me about it," I said. His testimony was that he was saved as a four year old boy. I asked him to relate to me what had happened, and he could not remember. "If you can't remember," I asked, "how can you know that you are saved?" "My mother told me that I prayed and reminds me that she knows that I am a Christian." Because of my doubts at this point, I gave him some literature about true salvation and asked him to read it. He did so and returned shortly with tears in his eyes. "Brother Binney," he said, "I am not a Christian. I have never been saved." After sharing a thorough presentation of the Gospel with him, he bowed his head and placed his complete trust and faith in Christ's death and resurrection. Amazingly, his disorder disappeared completely and instantly! What therapy could not do, salvation could. What medication could not do, Christ could. What the counselor could not do, the Holy Spirit could.

How frustrating it was for him to try to live as a Christian and fail constantly. How useless to treat him as a believer when he was not. How hopeful to finally find the means of spiritual victory which had eluded him!

I am convinced that this same challenge is faced by many parents. Attempting to rear a Christian child is an entirely different proposition than rearing an unsaved child. The unsaved child will naturally have more difficulties and struggles as their unregenerate spirit fights for the supremacy. Like an unbroken pony, they will kick against any efforts to tame them. But once the Holy Spirit of God puts a saddle on them and bends their will to His, even a wild pony can become a pleasure to behold.

Unfortunately, there are many who profess faith in

Christ who simply have not experienced it. Many of the people in our churches and homes today have never genuinely been saved. In fact, one prominent evangelist has estimated that over 50% of the members of Baptist churches are not even saved! Other leaders place the figure even higher! This phenomenon is not new. Jesus Himself spoke of this in His Sermon on the Mount:

"Enter ye in at the strait gate: for wide is the gate, and broad is the way, that leadeth to destruction, and MANY there be which go in thereat...Not every one that saith unto me, Lord, Lord, shall enter into the kingdom of heaven; but he that doeth the will of my Father which is in heaven. MANY will say to me in that day, Lord, Lord, have we not prophesied in thy name? And in thy name have cast out devils? and in thy name done many wonderful works? Ant then will I profess unto them, I never knew you: depart from me, ye that work iniquity." (Matthew 7:13, 21-23)
[Emphasis added]

My wife Sandra was reared in a godly Christian home. She attended a premier Gospel-preaching church and was exposed to the plan of salvation constantly throughout her childhood. Yet we had been married only a few months when she came to me and expressed doubts about her salvation. She was not sure she was saved. Despite her wonderful childhood, hearing great preaching, even attending a Bible college, she had disconcerting doubts which plagued her and robbed her of peace. How well I remember kneeling beside our bed with an open Bible and reading the wonderful truths of redemption together. We held hands and prayed and Sandra found the full assurance for which she had so longed.

   While I was a pastor, a man in our church came to my study for an appointment. As we began to talk, he began to tremble and to cry. "Pastor," he sobbed, "I am not sure that I am really saved. I have been plagued by doubts and I must find an answer!" I shared some scriptures with him and he prayed the sweetest, childlike prayer I had ever heard from an adult man. He arose from his knees with the joy of Jesus upon his face. He was a changed man! He had found Christ for the first time, even though he had been in church for years. The next Sunday he came forward in the church service to make his decision public. After he had testified of his new-found faith, it was revealed that there were others in our church with the same uncertainty and doubts. Within three months nineteen of our faithful church members had genuinely trusted Christ for the first time.

   How is it possible for a person to be wrong on the most important issue facing them, especially when they are immersed in the Bible teaching about it, and surrounded by people who promote it? How can a child grow up in a Christian home and attend a Bible-preaching church and lack assurance? Worse, lacking faith in God at all!? I will offer some thoughts on this subject in this chapter, but I would strongly urge every reader to read the article in the Appendices entitled "Can Church Members go to Hell?" for a fuller treatment of this question.

A Reliance upon Feelings

A seeker can be as easily misled by the presence of euphoric feelings as he can be by their absence. False salvation is often traced to one of these extremes. On the one hand, a person has a false hope based on a rush of emotion at the time of his "conversion," while another many struggle with doubts because of their absence. It is to the misleading conversion experience feelings that we will look for this writing, since we are considering a false salvation rather than false doubts. (For more information on this subject, I recommend my book "Blessed Assurance".)

Many times when the invitation to salvation is extended to children, it is accompanied by moving music, tearful penitents around him, and preceded by a moving presentation of the Gospel itself, as well as powerful motivations to make a decision on the spot. These things in combination can produce some powerful emotions.

Following a decision, there is often a rush of feelings as well. While often legitimate and therefore unimpeachable, one must question whether all emotions are indeed God-given. Is it possible for the deceiver to manufacture them? If he can deceive the nations of the world through signs and wonders, there is evidence that he can synthetically produce even "good" feelings. This is the meaning of "wonders"; it is the effect upon the observer of signs which causes him to have feelings of reverence, awe, and even admiration. Much of what passes for love today is little more than a skillful manipulation of immature hearts into feelings, which they interpret as genuine love. The moment of conversion is a prime time for him to inject these feelings, both as an object to seek, and as an evidence that you found true salvation.

Reliance Upon a Faulty Approach

I am absolutely convinced that many professing Christians are false believers because they have followed an incomplete approach, one designed for ease of understanding. Little children in children's ministries are exposed to Gospel invitations which, while intending to simplify salvation on the front end, actually complicate it terribly on the back end. Invitations to "ask Jesus into your heart," for example, while presented with a word picture of Jesus standing at the door and knocking, are meant to encourage the young to "accept Christ," or "invite Him into your life." If the reliance is upon this concept, a problem arises; we are not saved by accepting Christ, we are saved by Christ accepting us. While it is not wrong to pray a prayer to accept Him, it is wrong to rely on the concept or the prayer itself rather than coming to Christ with a full dependence upon His role in the process. (Please see the article, "A Scriptural Evaluation of Salvation Invitations" in the Appendices)

Reliance Upon a Formula Prayer

Compounding the problem is the well-intentioned but misguided practice of giving the child the precise words to pray at the time of conversion. It is assumed that by doing this, the young who are inexperienced in praying will be encouraged to say the right things. Again this is not wrong in itself, but if there is one scintilla of trust in the words spoken as a means to salvation, compared to the attitude of the heart, God's plan for a child can be derailed at the most crucial time of the process. Far better for the child to stumble through a less than perfect prayer, but one which reflects the true attitude of his heart, than be dictated a rote prayer from someone else's heart.

What is Needed

While effusive emotions, verbatim prayers, and even incomplete invitations need to be examined, their presence notwithstanding, a child can truly be saved IF one thing is present in tandem with them.

The Apostle Paul writes: *"That we should be to the praise of his glory, who first **trusted** in Christ. In whom ye also **trusted**, after that ye heard the word of truth, the gGospel of your salvation: in whom also, after that ye believed, ye were sealed with that holy Spirit of promise" (Ephesians 1:12-13).* The issue is trust. Where is the trust of the seeker focused? Upon what are they trusting? More to the point, in whom are they trusting?

The "believe" that is so essential in the salvation experience is qualified by its grammar and its context. The meaning of the word is "to rely upon, to lean your weight upon," or to "place your trust in," and goes farther than a mere mental assent to a fact. Both trusting Christ and receiving Christ are synonymous with believing. Both the grammar and the context of the above passage above demonstrate that the meaning of believe is to trust.

The danger comes when the trust is partial or misdirected, and this can happen if one is trusting their prayer or their feelings. To the degree that one trusts in anything but the finished work of Christ, the conversion is affected. Truly, to come to God with anything short of a "whole heart" of trust in Him is to negate the conversion.

Examining a Child's Salvation

When I question a counselee's salvation, I make every attempt to insure that they are, in fact, saved. I understand that it is not my role to judge their experience, but it is my responsibility to make every effort to insure its authenticity. In doing this, I take a couple of approaches which can be used by any parent.

Listen to Their Testimony

Without putting any words in their mouth, I simply ask, "Can you tell me how you became a Christian?" Then I listen very carefully. I am looking for expressions of trust, whether by concept or by use of the word "trust" itself. I want to know that this person is actively, consciously, and presently trusting nothing and nobody for their salvation but Christ and His finished work on the cross. I am cautious when I hear only such expressions as "I asked Jesus to come into my heart" with no reference to trusting Him. It is certainly okay to use this term if it is clear that it is accompanied by a evident trust and lively faith. But if all I hear is "I asked Jesus to come into my heart" with no reference to trust and faith, such a testimony is suspect, to say the least. If I am not completely satisfied, I move on to another question.

Ask Them to Tell You How You Can Be Saved.

I tell the person, "Imagine for a moment that I am lost. I have never been in a church and know absolutely nothing about the Bible, but I want to become a Christian. What would you tell me to do?" Again, I listen carefully. And again I am looking for the trust factor. If it is missing again, my suspicions mount.

I remember asking a man how he had become a Christian. He responded by merely saying, "I asked Jesus to come into my heart." When I asked him the follow-up question of what he would tell me I must do to be saved, he responded again, "By asking Jesus into your heart." As it turned out, he had never really been saved. All he understood about salvation was asking Jesus into your heart. He had been taught this as a child by a children's worker at church, and he had prayed with incomplete trust. As a result, he struggled with doubts about his salvation for years.

What's a Parent to Do?

In the case of doubts about your child's salvation, the wise parent will understand the need to give the Holy Spirit time to work in their young heart. Every Christian parent aches to know of their child's spiritual state, and longs for them to trust Christ, but be careful that in your desire that you don't rush the process.

With amazing consistency, great Christians of the past struggled with the question of their salvation. Sometimes for week, months, and even years, they agonized over their soul's condition. When they finally did break through into the light of assurance, it was a great day indeed!

While salvation is quick, it's not fast. One can be born in moments, but only after a pregnancy of nine months. One can be born again in moments, but only after a gradual work of the Spirit and truth upon the heart. We dare not eliminate the pregnancy in our rush for the birth. To shorten the pregnancy may produce a preemie who struggles for a lifetime.

The process of solid growth and change is outlined in Romans 6:17. (See "The Biblical Path to Lasting Change" in appendices.) It begins with doctrine which is understood with the intellect. Then it percolates down into the heart where it is assimilated and embraced as a passionate conviction. From there it moves to the will and out the life resulting in a changed behavior. Paul said, *"Ye have obeyed* (the will) *from the heart that form of doctrine* (the intellect) ." For the truth to travel from the head to the heart takes time. To by-pass the head for the heart is a major mistake and portends some serious problems for the future. Furthermore, to mistake a superficial feeling for a true conviction is a mistake as well.

Give the child time to ask questions and even struggle with doubts (as painful as it is to watch), till he comes to the point where he is "fully persuaded in [his] own mind", and "believes in [his] heart". Pray for him and with him for the full assurance he needs, but avoid the temptation of rushing the process.

At the same time, be aware of the tendency of your child to place his faith in his feelings instead of the truth. Most people I counsel who have doubts about their salvation struggle because they have valued their feelings over God's Word as the evidence of true salvation. In essence, their emotions have become an idol of the heart. They have more confidence in how they feel than in what God says.

In the final analysis, God is the only One who can determine the outcome. It is beyond the pay grade of any parent either to change a heart or to declare it changed. For that reason, it is imperative that you pray for the soul of your child. The Bible is clear that God is sensitive to the heart cry of parents, and His ears are open unto your cries.

Chapter Three

Goals for Christian Parenting

In any consideration about child rearing, every parent must make a clear distinction between goals and desires. In doing this, it is helpful to make three distinct comparisons: a comparison between capability, personal responsibility, and response. For example a *goal* is something you are capable of accomplishing, something for which you are responsible: the response to a goal is *action*. A *desire*, on the other hand, is something you are not capable of achieving and therefore not responsible to accomplish. Therefore, your response to a desire is *prayer*.

This distinction is emphasized in Psalm 37: *"Trust in the Lord, and do good; so shalt thou dwell in the land, and verily thou shalt be fed." (vs. 3).* The reader is shown the difference between "doing good" and "being fed." Doing good is a goal, being fed is a desire. How is the desire to be achieved? By "trusting in the Lord." The reader is responsible for doing good, God is responsible for the feeding. The Psalmist continues this thought in the same passage: *"Delight thyself also in the Lord;* (a goal) *and he shall give thee the desires of thine heart* (a desire). *Commit thy way unto the Lord;* (goal) *trust also in him;* (goal) *and he shall bring it to pass* (desire.)*" (vs. 4-5).*

When it comes to bringing up your child, every parent needs to make the distinction between a goal and a desire. Why is this so important? Because **when it comes to the mind, heart or will of another human being, nobody has the responsibility or capability of changing them!** That is a goal only God is able to accomplish. *"For it is God which worketh in you both to will and to do of his good pleasure." (Philippians 2:13). "The king's heart is in the hand of the Lord, as the rivers of water: he turneth it whithersoever he will" (Proverbs 21:1).* Think about it! From birth to death, a sovereign God is in control of your child. His life was planned by God before he was ever born. *"My substance was not hid from thee...Thine eyes did see my substance, yet being unperfect; and in thy book all my members were written, which in continuance were fashioned, when as yet there was none of them." (Psalm 139:15-16).* His salvation is initiated by Him. *"No man can come to me, except the Father which hath sent me draw him..." (John 6:44).*

Why is this true? Because man is so wicked and depraved, it is against his very nature even to seek God on his own without His help. *"As it is written, There is none righteous, no, not one: There is none that understandeth, there is none that seeketh after God. They are all gone out of the way, they are together become unprofitable; there is none that doeth good, no, not one...There is no fear of God before their eyes." (Romans 3:10-12, 18).* To complicate matters, your child's mind is blinded by Satan *"...lest the light of the*

28

glorious gospel of Christ ... should shine unto them" (2 Corinthians 4:4), and he is under Satan's control. *"And you hath he quickened,* (made alive) *who were dead in trespasses and sins; Wherein in time past ye walked according to the course of this world, according to the prince of the power of the air, the spirit that now worketh in the children of disobedience." (Ephesians 2:1-2).* Now, I ask you, what chance does your child ever have of being saved without the power and intervention of God Himself?! Why, even the very faith needed to be saved is a gift from Him. *"For by grace are ye saved through faith; and <u>that not of yourselves:</u>* (referring to the antecedent "faith") *it is the gift of God: Not of works lest any man should boast." (Ephesians 2:8-9)* Why? Because he does not have the wherewithal to "work it up!"

Now, here's the point of all these musings; if you have no control over your child's birth or salvation, and if only God could perform these things in his life, who is ultimately responsible for them? Are you responsible or is God? If God is responsible for your child <u>and</u> capable of saving him and directing him, should not your energies be invested in appealing to God on your child's behalf more than trying to do God's work for Him?

This is not to say that you do not have a responsibility in the matter, nor is it to say that you do not wield a significant influence in your child's life, but rather that a clear understanding of the needed balance is required of each parent if he is to see spiritual growth in his child.

One of the delightful and encouraging promises of God to His children is that when we pray according to His will He hears us. *"And this is the confidence that we have in him, that, if we ask any thing according to his will, he heareth us." (I John 5:14).* What could be better than knowing that the God of Heaven actually hears your prayers? Knowing with all certainty that the God of Heaven will answer your prayers! *"And if we know that he hear us, whatsoever we ask, we know that we have the petitions that we desired of him." (I John 5:15).* Amen! and Amen!

The obvious question to ask at this point is, "How can you know that you are praying in the will of God?" When God reveals His will in His Word, we know it is His will. His will is obvious when we see that He has particular goals for His children. As parents, your great concern is for the goals He has for your children! Once you establish God's goals for your children, you can pray for the desires of your heart because now your desires and His goals are one.

If I were to ask you, "What is your purpose in the discipline and training of your child?" what would be your answer? What is your goal? Unfortunately, many parents merely want their children to behave so their behavior won't reflect poorly upon their parenting. Others desire to have children who will embrace their beliefs and convictions. Still others use discipline as a tool of revenge against children who have deprived them of cherished goals. Lesser goals may be merely the desire to maintain harmony in the home for the sake of peace.

Many parents have never really thought about goals or purposes in child rearing. It's the thing to do and expected of good parents in respectable circles, but the success of any venture is dependent upon a clearly stated purpose. Churches have mission statements, schools have a philosophy of education and core goals for each student, and businesses have financial goals of a good bottom line. Should parents have any less?

In considering your goals as parents, where can you go for a model? Psychologists will tell you the goal should be self-esteem, philosophers will point to knowledge, and the world will emphasize success. One can readily assume that the source of your goals will determine your goals. If that is true, where should the Christian parent turn? The answer to that is **the Word of God**!

There we find three primary goals which God has for your children. These goals, when incorporated into the parenting of your child, can make the difference between God's blessing upon your child and failure. What are they?

GOAL #1: INDEPENDENCE

"For this cause shall a man leave his father and mother, and shall be joined unto his wife, and they two shall be one flesh." Ephesians 5:31

From birth to death, God is at work in each of us to prepare us to live independently of our parents. This break is necessary to insure the formation of a new family unity. The ultimate goal for every parent is to work themselves out of a job! If you have done your job right, your child will gradually be equipped and trained to make it on his own. For many parents, this is a hard realization to face. They hate the thought of little junior ever growing up they think of him as their "baby," and find it difficult to imagine living without him or envisioning him as able to make it on his own. As a result, they have never made the commitment to prepare their child for independence. They fail to formulate a plan for such a lofty goal.

This issue must be faced by you if you are to agree with God about His purpose for your child. His goal for your child is independence from you – not from your fellowship but from your control and provision. To fail to make this your goal is to disqualify yourself to pray in the will of God for the future of your child. Make it your purpose that you will prepare your child to live without you. Your greatest legacy to your child may be his preparation for independence. But you must have this clearly defined in your heart before you can accomplish it.

GOAL #2: PERSONAL RESPONSIBILITY

"So then every one of us shall give account of himself to God." Romans 14:12

Any goal of parenting must include the teaching of individual responsibility to children. In an age when blame-shifting and excuse-making have been elevated to a fine art, it is absolutely imperative that youth acquire the character to shoulder the responsibility for their own actions and choices.

The victim mentality will not go far when they stand before God to "give account of themselves." Mom won't be there nor will Dad; just junior with a naked soul and a private burden. Preparing them for that should be the priority of every parent.

It is important to teach a child the value of hard, manual labor. *"It is good for a man that he bear the yoke in his youth."(Lamentations 3:27).* Insuring that he has daily chores, and even works a hard, dirty, sweaty job is good for their sense of responsibility. I have a dear friend who is very wealthy, and yet he required his daughters to work cleaning houses and doing other chores while they were growing up. He wanted them to value a dollar and know the importance of hard work.

Teaching that fun times always follow work times, such as chores, homework, etc. will also instill habits of responsible behavior.

Enforced labors at unpleasant tasks build character in a child. Staying at homework until its finished and practicing the piano every day are examples of this.

Other ways of teaching responsibility are insuring that he always admits wrongdoing without blame-shifting, teaching that incomplete obedience is disobedience, teaching fiscal responsibility, and discouraging criticism of others, especially spiritual authorities.

GOAL #3: HOLINESS

"Furthermore we have had fathers of our flesh which corrected us, and we gave them reverence: shall we not much rather be in subjection unto the Father of spirits, and live? For they verily for a few days chastened us after their own pleasure; but he for our profit, that we might be partakers of his holiness. Now no chastening for the present seemeth to be joyous, but grievous: nevertheless afterward it yieldeth the peaceable fruit of righteousness unto them which are exercised thereby." Hebrews 12:9-11

It can readily be seen that the goal of God in disciplining His children is that they acquire His holiness and enjoy the fruits of righteousness. Our purpose in parenting must reflect this rather than our "own pleasure."

The scriptural way of teaching this holiness to your child is to direct them to God's holiness. His holiness is the motive of theirs. *"But as he which hath called you is holy, so be ye holy in all manner of conversation; Because it is written, Be ye holy; for I am holy." (1 Peter 1:15-16)* Teaching the holiness of God is the ultimate means of helping your child acquire his own holiness.

Another way of helping your child acquire holiness is to model it for him. Children are master imitators. Because they want so badly to be like Mom or Dad, they will pick up your habits. How important, then, to give them the right habits to copy. If they see you praying, they will pray. If they watch you reading your Bible, they will want one of their own. If they observe you witnessing, they will tell their little friends about Jesus. What joy I had as a young preacher to watch my son swinging his little arms in imitation of our song leader and set up a chair in our living room for a pulpit while he preached like his daddy.

And, of course, the ultimate way of helping your child to be godly is to help him to be *"conformed to the image of His Son" (Romans 8:29)*. As they learn about Christ, they see the very character of God modeled at the highest level. As they receive the Son of God as their personal Savior, they receive the Spirit within them to aid them into becoming more Christlike.

None of this is possible, however, until and unless your child is led to the place of actually trusting the Lord Jesus Christ as his personal Savior. The prayer of every parent should be for the early salvation of his child. Praying for his salvation, exposing him to the Gospel at every opportunity, and witnessing effectively to him are godly goals that a parent can pursue to help his child learn of God's holiness.

Conclusion

So the balance between goals and desires is vitally important in the fine art of parenting. Your prayers should reflect your absolute dependence upon God, and your actions should reflect your trust in God to bless your efforts at accomplishing His will in your child's life. If your goals are His goals, then your prayers for your child will be in His will, you can understand your role as distinctly different from His role, and He will enable you as His steward to accomplish His will as a parent. You will also be dependent upon Him for the ultimate outcome of your child's life. When this balance is in place, you can rest in His strength.

Chapter Four

Balancing the Rod

Any consideration about the biblical teaching on child discipline must be preceded by a balanced approach to the matter. In a sincere desire to do the right thing, too much of a good thing can undo the good you desire. Much of the Christian life is learning to balance our living. The letter of the law must be balanced with the spirit of the law; truth with love; liberty with restraint, evangelism with discipleship, etc.

Balance is particularly needed in the sphere of child discipline, especially in the key areas of Control vs. Love, "Nurture" vs. "Admonition," and Influence vs. Cause.

A Balance Between Love and Control
"Speaking the truth in love..." Ephesians 4:15

Within many families there is a dramatic disparity in the parenting styles of the father and mother. This may be the result of differences in their own upbringings. One of them, brought up in a harsh environment, may favor a tender, merciful, loving approach to discipline of the children. Another, in reaction to permissive parents, may be determined to help (or make) their children avoid the excesses of libertarianism. They bring the hammer down and insist on their children toeing the line.

These and other differences are dramatically illustrated in a study done by some graduate students interested in gauging the results of varied approaches of parenting on the lifestyles of teenagers.[1] Their goal was to determine why some young people do not follow the religious convictions of their parents. To accomplish this, they asked several hundred teens to rate their parents in two specific categories: the expression of love and the expression of control Each category could be rated from 1 to 100 to measure intensity.

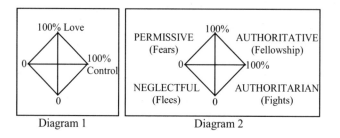

Diagram 1   Diagram 2

Four basic parenting styles soon emerged which reflected the findings of diagram #1.

Neglectful - low in love, low in control This type of parent avoids or *flees* his children.

Permissive - high in love, low in control. This parent allows his children to lead him rather than leading them. He *fears* his children. Often this fear is one of losing their love.

Authoritarian - low in love, high in control. This parent pushes his children to conform to his military standards with no exceptions and no excuses! He *fights* his children.

Authoritative - high in love, high in control. This parent *fellowships* with his children.

Diagram #2 shows an overview of these findings.

The results of the survey were then tabulated to rate the response of the teens to each parenting style in several categories. These categories measured the teens' responses to authority, acceptance of their parents' religious beliefs, and acceptance of their parents' lifestyle. The question of which parenting style they were most responsive toward was addressed.

I. Response to "Authority"
    Authoritative
    Permissive
    Neglectful
    Authoritarian

    Conclusion: Motivation to want to obey (rather than being forced to obey) encourages obedience to authority.

II. Acceptance of Parents' Religion
    Authoritative
    Permissive
    Neglectful
    Authoritarian

Conclusion: Children brought up in religious homes tend to embrace the ideals of authoritative parents, but reject those of authoritarian parents.

III. Acceptance of Parents' Lifestyle
Authoritative
Permissive
Neglectful
Authoritarian

Conclusion: Young people are prone to reject the lifestyles of "pushy," authoritarian parents, and follow that of the authoritative ones.

In each case, where love is present in balance with control, the child is better equipped to face life. This is not to negate the need of control but to demonstrate the need of balance. Many young parents, in their initial approach to child discipline, feel that control is the primary issue. Often they are living under a strict "letter of the law" teaching or preaching which encourages them to take a hard line for the child's good without being taught to balance control with love.

It is as foolish and counterproductive to force control onto a child in the absence of love as it is to speak the truth without love. The balance of teaching and love is well established in the Scriptures. *"That we henceforth be no more children…But speaking the truth in love, may grow up into him in all things…" (Ephesians 4:14-15).* Just as members of harsh, oppressive churches can become disillusioned with Christianity and "burn out," so children in harsh, oppressive homes can react with disillusionment.

If this study indicates anything, it shows the need of love, the importance of balance, and the danger of undue control in the life of a child.

A Balance Between "Nurture" and "Admonition"
"And, ye fathers, provoke not your children to wrath: but bring them up in the nurture and admonition of the Lord."
Ephesians 6:4

In giving this admonition to the church at Ephesus, the Apostle Paul was exhorting them to maintain a balance between "nurture" and "admonition." To fail in this can "provoke" the child to wrath. Who can know of the vast amounts of wrath, anger, and bitterness which are traceable to an abusive childhood? Often in my counseling I have been called upon to help a wounded spirit deal with a lifetime of anger because of insensitive parents who lost the balance.

Paul's emphasis here is a balance between *"nurture"* and *"admonition."* "Nurture" refers to training from the outside to the inside. This is teaching in the form of discipline imposed from the will of the parent to that of the child. This same word is translated "chasten" in Hebrews chapter 12. It means literally to "train by rules and regulations" and carries the idea of enforcing this training through rewards and discipline. This kind of training focuses on the actions of the child rather than his beliefs. The principle here is that actions produce attitudes. *"Commit thy*

41

works (actions) *unto the Lord, and thy thoughts* (attitudes) *shall be established." (Proverbs 16:3).*

The reason for this in small children is that they do not possess the capacity to reason through the rights and wrongs of issues. *"Foolishness is bound in the heart of a child..."* Although they may not understand right and wrong, they can understand pain and pleasure, *"...but the rod of correction shall drive it far from him." (Proverbs 22:15).* To nurture a child means that he is brought up in an environment of clear rules, the violation of which brings pain. The consistent application of biblical nurturing in the early years insures the reception of admonition.

"Admonition," on the other hand, has the meaning of training from the inside to the outside. Just as nurture begins on the outside and moves to the inside of the child, so admonition works from the inside to the outside. While nurture trains the will through imposed discipline, admonition trains the mind and heart through acquired truth. The result is a balanced child.

Admonition is traceable to the Greek word "nouthesia" which means a verbal instruction with a view to correct. An entire system of Christian counseling has arisen in America called "Nouthetic Counseling." The emphasis behind nouthetic counseling is to confront and teach with truth.

An imbalance of nurture and admonition is disastrous. Nurture without admonition means that the parent imposes his will upon his child with little thought to helping him to be "fully persuaded" in his own mind. By use of an iron-fisted system of unquestionable rules and regulations, the parent makes the child toe the line and spout the party line of parental standards with no room for independent thought or sincere questions. Such parents are shocked when their children leave home and abandon every standard under which they have lived their entire life. One reason for this is that many youth have grown up resenting the harsh restraints and have merely bided their time until they could break free! They were never convinced! It was never their standard! They were never fully persuaded in their own minds but rather in the minds of their parents! They never had a chance to think or voice their sincere questions as such actions were tantamount to insubordination! Their lives were controlled by the wills of the parents, and they never developed convictions of their own … other than the conviction that "When I have kids, I'll let them have their liberty!"

The other extreme of imbalance is admonition without nurture. When the child acquires biblical knowledge without self restraint, he is set up for a presumptuous lifestyle. For example, here is a child who is taught about forgiveness without learning discipline through nurture. He quickly learns that all he has to do is ask forgiveness and all is forgiven. So he thinks to himself, "I will sin all I want today, but before I go to bed, I will ask forgiveness and all will be well." As an adult, he may max out his credit card because he has been taught that the rapture could occur any day. Extreme? Perhaps, but I have known of such thinking which was the result of admonition without nurture.

Balancing nurture and admonition has much to do with

timing. This may be reflected in the order of placement of these words in Ephesians 6:4. Notice that as nurture precedes admonition in the verse, so it should receive the heaviest emphasis in the early years of a child. As the child matures, less nurture is needed and more admonition is called for. The ultimate goal of maturity is an adult who is led by admonition almost exclusively. This is achieved over the span of a child's life by the gradual displacement of nurture by admonition. (See Diagram 3)

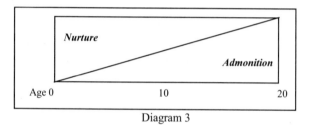

Diagram 3

A Balance Between Influence and Cause

"Train up a child in the way he should go: and when he is old, he will not depart from it." Proverbs 22:6
"So then every one of us shall give account of himself to God." Romans 14:12

Every parent has an influence on their children. For good or for bad, you leave an impression.

You are responsible for your influence and you will answer to God for any failure to exert a godly influence over your children. You should pray with them, teach them the Bible, witness to them, discipline them in love, enroll them in

Sunday school, take them to church, be a godly example, etc. If you fail in this, you need to confess it to God, and possibly to your children as well; but in the final analysis, your child must stand on his own two feet and give account for his own decisions.

This is the difference between Proverbs 22:6 and Romans 14:12 which on the surface seem contradictory. *"Train up a child"* refers to your influence as a parent, *"... everyone shall give account of himself"* refers to personal choice as the cause of every person's behavior.

It preaches really well on the front end of a child's life to emphasize the need of parents to train their children correctly, but to preach it out of balance can result in misplaced guilt. If the parents' role is stressed too much on the back end of the child's life, twenty to thirty years later, the parents are guilt-ridden, and the child is guilt-free and angry at his parents for making such a mess out of his life. On the other hand, if personal choice is over emphasized, parents can easily dismiss their response out of hand.

By seeing the difference between an influence and cause in their child's life, parents will approach child rearing with a balanced concern for parental influence and their child's responsibility.

Conclusion

Extremism is the product of truth out of balance. We see this extremism all around us, even in the church ... and especially in the home. Any biblical principles brought to bear upon the issue of child rearing must be used in a Spirit-controlled balance and consistency to maximize their effect upon the child.

Maintaining a balance in the areas of love and control, nurture and admonition, and influence and cause will go far in strengthening your role as a parent and encouraging your child toward godliness.

Footnotes:

[1]Hindson, Edward, *The Total Family*, Tyndale, 1980, pp. 56-60.

Chapter Five

Nine Steps to Child Discipline

As in any venture, the absence of a plan evokes fear. Christians fear to witness because they don't have a method; counselors fear to counsel because they lack a strategy, while others fear to teach because they have never learned a system of studying and presenting the truth. When it comes to parenting, such fear can be paralyzing.

As I reflect back on my early days of fatherhood, I can only claim ignorance to the extreme. For instance, I was worried about how I was ever going to teach my son to talk. I wondered how I could demonstrate the right shape of the lips, the contortion of the tongue, and the stimulation of the vocal cords to evoke language from him. The fear of teaching him how to talk, however, was soon replaced with a fear that he would never stop!

The icy fingers of fear have gripped the heart of many a parent while holding a tiny new baby for the first time and realizing, "It's up to me to bring this child up properly!" How do you overcome such fear? Like the soulwinner, the counselor, and the teacher, you need a plan.

The purpose of this chapter is to equip the parent with such a plan, a system of disciplining the wayward child and training him in righteousness. From the offense to the correction, nine biblical, practical and sequential steps are presented. Hopefully, the results of this are that by having a plan, much of the fear can be eliminated, and your child will experience the in-depth changes which God desires.

If you are a brand new parent, this information will be invaluable. If you have older children and you feel it is too late, take heart! The principles you are about to learn will help you as well.

STEP #1: SEND THE CHILD TO HIS ROOM

By sending your child to his room, provision is made for several steps of spiritual preparation which insure the deepest possible working of God in his spirit.

First of all, sending him to his room to be alone allows the Holy Spirit of God time to work on his conscience. He needs to be encouraged to think about the possible damage he may have caused to others and to give some thought to how he has offended and sinned against God.

This time will also allow the child time to reflect upon the seriousness of what he has done. The goal here is not self -centered remorse but a *"godly sorrow"* which "worketh repentance" *(2 Corinthians 7:10)*. The Apostle Paul makes a distinction between merely having regrets for getting caught, sadness over experiencing a loss, shame from exposure, and pain from penalties and true "godly sorrow." When he wrote to the church at Corinth, he said to them, *"Now I rejoice, not that ye were made sorry, but that ye sorrowed to repentance: for ye were made sorry after a godly manner ... For godly sorrow worketh repentance .. but the sorrow of the world worketh death." (2 Corinthians 7:9-10).* A godly sorrow which worketh repentance must come from the Holy Spirit and result in an awful awareness of sin committed as well as the need to make it right. Giving your child time to reflect on these things will allow the Spirit opportunity to bring the burden of conviction upon him.

Another reason for this time alone for the child is to clearly establish a break of fellowship with you, his parent. The ultimate and consummate consequence of sin against our Heavenly Father is to experience the pain and agony of the loss of His fellowship. Although we never lose our blessed Father-child relationship with Him, we can lose the sweetness and intimacy of His presence.

When my son was small, I heard a dull "thunk" sound coming from the living room. To my dismay, I discovered him with a hammer in his hand and a hole in the fish tank. At his feet the last drops of water gurgled and bubbled through the fibers of the carpet where several goldfish writhed in frantic desperation. With an angelic look on his face, Jonathan proudly announced, "Daddy, I let dem fishies out!" Although I was aware of my relationship with my son, I knew our fellowship had been broken; and by the sinking countenance of my son, I could see that he knew it as well. This break in fellowship is an integral and vital part of the discipline process if it is to reflect God's way in dealing with us.

While your child is spending this time alone…

STEP #2: GET ALONE WITH GOD

A common mistake of parents is to deal too quickly with the sin of their child, to hasten the identification and punishment of his waywardness. A rush to judgment at this point can be dangerous. By sending your child to his room and finding some solitude for yourself, you are providing time for some important preparations.

This allows you time to "cool off." Hasty discipline leads to regrets on the part of the parent and may *"provoke ... your [child] to wrath." (Ephesians 6:4)*. *"He that is slow to wrath is of great understanding: but he that is hasty of spirit exalteth folly." (Proverbs 14:29)*. Restraint at this point is very definitely the better part of wisdom. *"Wherefore, my beloved brethren, let every man be swift to hear, slow to speak, slow to wrath: For the wrath of man worketh not the righteousness of God." (James 1:19-20)*.

More than once I have found myself struggling with feelings of anger over the sin of my child. I wish that I could say that I exercised restraint on each of these occasions, but unfortunately, at times I fear I was guilty of "exalting folly" through a hasty spirit.

Not only does a hasty approach fail to work righteousness, it also creates tension in the relationship. *"A soft answer turneth away wrath: but grievous words stir up anger." (Proverbs 15:1)*.

This time apart from your child gives you some needed time to approach God in humble prayer for wisdom and guidance. I marvel at the ignorance with which we, as parents, approach this challenging task called parenting. It is of the highest order, requiring the greatest of knowledge and wisdom, and yet of all professions, it seems that any training we receive is "on-the-job." Even a dog catcher or plumber receives some training before going to work, but a parent is left to his own devices with no diploma or degree in parenting. It seems he is destined to bang around in the dark in hopes of finding a solution.

God has a salvation for you. He gives you "directions for assembly" called the Bible, and He promises you the answers you need when you need them. *"If any of you lack wisdom, let him ask of God, that giveth to all men liberally, and upbraideth not; and it shall be given him." (James 1:5).* This, of all times, is a time when you need wisdom.

The second reason for prayer is to appeal to God to work His conviction upon the heart of your child. By the power of your personality and the force of your will, you can strike fear into his heart; but you, as a human, can never accomplish what only God can do. *"... it is God which worketh in you* [and in your child] *both to will and to do of his good pleasure." (Philippians 2:13).* Notice it is God who has the power to move upon your child's will. Furthermore, He holds the very heart of your child in His sovereign hand and can turn it in any direction He desires. *"The king's heart is in the hand of the Lord, as the rivers of water: he turneth it whithersoever he will." (Proverbs 21:1).*

This is not a reference to huge rivers like the Ohio or Mississippi but about irrigation ditches commonly found on the lands of farmers in Bible days. The same source of water fed the back forty acres as the front forty, and the flow was controlled by a gate which could be maneuvered to direct the water in the direction the farmer desired. By pulling a lever, he could funnel the water as he pleased. God has His hand on the lever of your child's heart. He can direct it in any direction He pleases. He is in absolute control. That is why it is so important for you to appeal to Him and rely on Him to bring conviction and change into the heart of your child. These few moments of imposed solitude will go far in preparing your child for lasting change.

STEP #3: QUESTION YOUR CHILD

The temptation of the novice parent is to charge wildly at the child with a pre-established list of accusations against him: "You lied!" "You stole that!" "You hit your sister!" and other charges are made posthaste with disastrous results. It is a truism that "Accusations attack the will, but questions prick the conscience." The conscience is the target at this point, not the will. The only effect of strong accusations on the will is to harden it into resistance and rebellion, making it more difficult for any deep change to occur. It is far better to approach the child with some key questions to guide his thinking into conformity with God's.

The Lord Jesus Christ gives us a pattern to follow. He skillfully used a series of questions to help His listeners arrive at a predetermined conclusion. He knew where He wanted them to go; but rather than pushing them there with accusations, He led them with questions.

On one occasion, Jesus had gone into a synagogue on the Sabbath day to teach. He spotted a man whose right hand was withered and in need of healing. The self-righteous scribes and Pharisees who were present wanted to accuse Him of sin and tried to trap Him. *"... And they asked him saying, Is it lawful to heal on the sabbath days? that they might accuse him." (Matthew 12:10).* At this point, Jesus could have told them exactly what He intended to do, or for that matter, simply have healed the man outright. Instead, He skillfully posed some incremental, progressive questions which convicted their consciences. *"And he said unto them, What man shall there be among you, that shall have one sheep, and if it fall into a pit on the sabbath day, will he not lay hold on it, and lift it out? How much then is a man better than a sheep?" (vs. 11-12).* By asking these questions, He confronted them with the truth He wanted them to learn. After this preparation, *"Then saith he to the man, Stretch forth thine hand' And he stretched it forth; and it was restored whole, like as the other." (vs. 13).* The conclusion was inescapable; the will of God was for the man to be healed; but Christ wanted to address the conscience of the witnesses.

A wise parent will emulate our Lord in this approach. You may know the violation of which your child is guilty, and you may know the ultimate conclusion you desire him to form. By leading him through some well thought out questions to form his own conclusions, you allow the Spirit of God to convict him of sin. "Johnny, what did you say about your sister?" "Was that a true statement?" "If it wasn't a true statement, what kind of statement was it?" "What does God call that?" "Did you tell a lie?" "How does God feel about lying?" "What do you feel is the right thing to do now?" "It's good that you want to seek God's forgiveness. Is there anyone else whose forgiveness you need?" "Do you think you should seek your sister's forgiveness, too?"

STEP #4: REINFORCE BIBLICAL PRINCIPLES

Principles are different than rules. Principles are broad, overarching truths which apply in many situations while rules are designed to deal with a specific situation. For example, it is one thing to say "Don't smoke!" It is quite another to teach the principle of God's ownership of your body and the importance of glorifying Him in everything you do with your body. The principle of ownership includes smoking but is not limited to it. It also includes drinking, drugs, illicit sex, gluttony, anorexia, bulimia, tattooing, body piercing and other sins against the body.

No wise parent should avoid handing down a judgment or fail to address any of the particular sins listed above, but the question is, how do you address them? At some point, of course, you will have to give a firm "yes" or "no," but the biblically savvy parent will have more to base his response upon than a weak "Because I said so! That's why!" He can bring his decision under the umbrella of what God says and bring the full authority of God's wishes to bear on the issue at hand.

Paul taught that lasting change comes from obedience which comes from the heart which is traceable to the head. *"But God be thanked, that ye were the servants of sin but ye have obeyed from the heart that form of doctrine which was delivered you." (Romans 6:17).* Teaching and applying biblical principles is powerful admonition which in time will be embraced by the heart and lived out in the life.

STEP #5: DISCIPLINE UNTIL THE WILL IS BROKEN

Essential to any discussion on the subject of corporal punishment (spanking) is a clear understanding of what biblical discipline is. The Bible terms include "chastening," "nurture," etc. *"For whom the Lord loveth he chasteneth, and scourgeth every son whom he receiveth...for our profit, that we might be partakers of his holiness" (Hebrews 12:6,10).*

The word "chastening" suggests "the broad ideas of education ... instructing ... training ... to chastise with blows, to scourge ... suggesting that Christian discipline regulates character..."[3] The goal of spanking is to instill Christian character, to train the child. The means is physical pain and discomfort.

"Discipline" not "Punishment"

There is a basic difference between this discipline and what is commonly called punishment. Discipline is always done out of love, punishment is often done out of anger. Discipline is for the good of the offender, punishment is for the satisfaction of the one administering the strokes. Discipline is with an eye to the future, punishment is with an eye to the past. Discipline always instills hope, punishment is more likely to instill despair. Discipline promotes holiness, punishment can promote anger.

Use a Neutral Object

Nowhere in the Scriptures is the parent instructed to use his hand in the disciplining process. The Bible promotes the use of the "rod," a word with the various meanings of "a slender and flexible shoot or twig, a branch or bough, a staff for walking, a shepherd's crook used in tending his flock, and the scepter of a king as an emblem of power."[4]

The general meaning conveyed is that this is an object used to represent authority and inflict pain. It is significant that the use of the rod is promoted while the use of the hand is not. I believe the reason for this is that the child should associate his pain with a neutral object rather than a part of his parent's body. One small child was seen carrying his daddy's paddle out of the house. "Where are you going with that, son?" his father asked. "I'm going to throw it away." replied the boy. "Why do you want to do that?" "Because I hate it!" Far better for the child to hate the rod than the parent.

Hide Your Face During the Spanking

During the process of the spanking, it is wise for the parent to insure that the child does not witness the grimace of the parent's efforts or any expressions which could be interpreted as anger or uncontrolled rage. From a sensitive child's position and perspective, this could inflict a greater wound than the physical suffering. It is the child's actions which are rejected not the child himself, and he does not need to be confused by any images which might signal otherwise. Even God the Father hid His face from the Son on the cross. *"In a little wrath I hid my face from thee for a moment; but with everlasting kindness will I have mercy on thee, saith the LORD thy Redeemer." (Isaiah 54:8)*

Continue Only Briefly Beyond the Child's Brokenness

An ever-present danger in this process is that of extremes in the discipline. Too little pain produces rebellion. *"...let not thy soul spare for his crying" (Proverbs 19:18).* On the other hand, too much pain can create anger. *"...provoke not your children to wrath." (Ephesians 6:4).*

Finding the right balance can be tricky, but one indicator that the child's spirit is broken is that he stops resisting and demonstrates a yieldedness to his just deserts. Squirming, screaming and bawling replaced by sobbing is one evidence. It is vital not to go too far beyond this point.

Some suggest that the child be told precisely how many strokes will be administered, but this assumes that all children are created equal when it comes to discipline. It is important to adjust the duration, style and intensity of any discipline to fit the temperament of the child. For some, a look, a word, or at most a stroke or two is sufficient. For other children, this would be a cakewalk. Be flexible in adjusting to the individuality of each child.

All of us must learn to surrender our will to God's, but this is something that has to be learned. The godly parent is a key player in God's plan for teaching the child to do this. Chronic resistance to the parent's will conditions the child to resist God's will. But teaching the child to surrender to the will of the earthly father or spiritual authority will prepare him to better yield to that of the Heavenly Father.

STEP #6: ALLOW TIME FOR BROKENNESS

After the child has been thoroughly dealt with by the parent, he needs to be left alone for a period of reflection and brokenness. The full implications of his sinfulness rarely sink in immediately, but now that he has been questioned and has had biblical principles reinforced into his thinking, the Holy Spirit can use this time to impress upon him the exceeding sinfulness of his waywardness.

Another reason for this time of solitude is to bring to bear one of the often overlooked and undervalued needs of the disciplining process: a break in the parent-child relationship. The implications of this can best be seen at the cross.

The cross was a grievous burden for our Lord to bear. But one of its most painful aspects to Him was surprisingly not the physical pain but the break in fellowship with His Father. The Father had made Christ to become sin for us, and He could not look on His Son. For the first and only time in history, the fellowship between the Son and the Father was broken. This, far more than the physical suffering, was the agony of the cross for the Savior. *"...My God, my God, why hast thou forsaken me?" (Matthew 27:46)*

Leaving the child alone for a period of time will underscore the heaviness of his sin. The break of parental fellowship combined with the opportunity to feel the full weight of sin will produce a needed "godly sorrow unto repentance."

The song writer put it well: "He washed my eyes with tears that I might see..."

STEP #7: LOVE HIM

Your child needs to know that you hate what he did rather than hating him for what he did. He needs to know it is his actions being rejected and not his person. Sincere and warm expressions of your love will give him this assurance.

Hugs, kisses, touches and words will go far to bring healthy closure to the process. This sense of closure, of finalization is very important to the child.

The timing, however, is important. Making this the

seventh step is no accident. It is placed here to avoid the well -intentioned but premature expressions of love often shared with the child. It is a syrupy sentimentality which equates forgiveness with haste and instant assurances of love with mercy. Signs of love and forgiveness planted on the school yards of teen killers the day after their wicked shooting sprees send the wrong message. Extending love before repentance may be perceived as a sort of condonement of sin or even a pre-occupation with the needs of the offender over the victims, a mindset which led to the sin in the first place.

But at some point, a closure to the incident is needed to avoid leaving the child in a confused state of uncertain rejection with little hope of reconciliation with his parents and less understanding of how to accomplish it.

Expressions of parental love assure the child that the parent is addressing the act of his sin rather than locking him into a state of sin. By dealing with the specific sin and then granting forgiveness and love, it is clear to the child that the break in fellowship is temporary and not permanent. This will go far in equipping the child in the future to distinguish the difference between the loss of God's fellowship and His relationship.

The importance of loving your child was underscored in some recent long-term studies on child rearing. It was determined that in the final analysis, it is more important for the child to grow up and leave home with the pervasive sense of being loved than the perfect application of a grocery list of specific techniques. Don't lose sight of your child's need of knowing he is loved in your slavish devotion to a perfect application of techniques.

STEP #8: PRAY WITH HIM

The purpose of this time of prayer is to lead him in the biblical confession of his sin and to teach him to claim God's forgiveness.

The Biblical Confession of Sin

"If we confess our sins, he is faithful and just to forgive us our sins, and to cleanse us from all unrighteousness."
(1 John 1:9)

Contrary to politically correct thinking, seeking God's forgiveness does not require "asking for forgiveness." The key to understanding this is the word "confess" in the above passage. The Greek word is "HOMOLOGEO;" "HOMO" meaning "same," and "LOGEO" meaning word. Confession, then, means to say the same word as God says. This is a lost art in an age of a therapeutic vocabulary. Calling sinners "victims", for example, will never evoke a biblical process of confession. Neither will training a child to approach God in a way He does not promote. Rather than teaching him to ask God for forgiveness, he needs to learn to claim the offer of forgiveness already available. The way of claiming it is the act of confession. But claiming what is already offered is far different from asking.

Not since Calvary are we told to ask for forgiveness.

Because all the punishment for sin was met there, all the forgiveness we need is freely provided by the blood of Jesus Christ. This forgiveness is appropriated through confession.

The prayer of confession involves agreeing with God that what I am responsible for is a sin (not a mistake, someone else's fault, a lapse in judgment, etc.), agreeing with God that the sin is against Him and His Word, and agreeing with God by using the same language to describe my sin that He uses.

It may be necessary to coach your child in this process in the initial attempts at prayer, but time and experience will wean him from this. Have him pray first, then lead him into a fuller confession if the need exists, then you pray aloud for him.

STEP #9: LEAD HIM TO MAKE RESTITUTION

Zacchaeus was a publican or a tax collector. Publicans were especially despised by their fellow countrymen because they worked in consort with the hated Romans to exact taxes from them. Because Rome did not care how much the publicans kept for themselves as long as they collected the required amount, the publicans had no restraints on what they could demand while they enjoyed all the authority of Rome in collecting it. Needless to say, this made them very rich but also very unpopular.

Zacchaeus, who was not only a publican but "the chief among the publicans," had a change of heart when he met

Christ and desired to do the right thing. His repentance was so complete that it prompted him to declare, *"... Behold, Lord, the half of my goods I give to the poor; and if I have taken any thing from any man by false accusation, I restore him fourfold." (Luke 19:8).* Upon hearing these words, Christ declared, *"... This day is salvation come to this house..." (Luke 19:9).*

The principle of restitution taught in the Scriptures involves making right the damage done by one's sin. If your child stole something, have him return it; if he broke something, have him replace it; if he hurt someone, require that he make it right.

This is necessary in order for him to learn more fully of the consequences of his sin and his personal responsibility in correcting the damage it caused.

Conclusion

Don't lose sight of the purpose of all these steps. In the final analysis, the only purpose worthy of your efforts is God's purpose. He chastens us *"... that we might be partakers of His holiness." (Hebrews 12:10).* Keep this lofty goal before you and you will not lose heart, even in the midst of the tedious and chronic diligence required to help your child. Yes, there will be struggles and disappointments in the training of your child, *"...nevertheless afterward it yieldeth the peaceable fruit of righteousness unto them which are exercised thereby." (Hebrews 12:11).*

Footnotes:

[1] *Focus on the Family Magazine*, April 1998, p. 2.

[2] Ibid.

[3] Vine, W.E., *Expository Dictionary of New Testament Words,* 1966, p. 183.

[4] Wilson, William, *Old Testament Word Studies,* Kregel, Grand Rapids, 1978, p. 360.

Chapter Six

Praying for You Children

The world was shocked at the news of a mob attack on a Bible-preaching church in San Francisco, California! It happened in the very heart of the city at the Hamilton Square Baptist Church. A speaker invited by the pastor did not meet the approval of the local sodomite community. They rallied over 100 screaming homosexuals who surrounded the building and ran amuck in unrestrained riot. They trashed the property and lowered the American flag to replace it with the rainbow flag of the "Queer Nation."

"We want your children!"

As the church members arrived, the mob formed a gauntlet at the church entrance, forcing them to walk through the very heart of the tempest. They screamed at these frightened believers, even manhandling some of them. Once inside, the doors were bolted and the police called, but there was little response. Outside the mob was pounding on the doors and screaming invectives. Most chilling of all was the taunting chant, "We want your children!"

If the truth were known, the sodomites are not the only force wanting America's children. A missionary recently told me that he found three porno sites under child related addresses on the web. The tobacco industry has shown its true colors in the past, "Joe Camel" approach to seduce children. Television is awash in youthful programs featuring sex, the occult, and rebellion against authority. MTV is an ever-growing force among Christian young people as evidenced by the fact that 42 percent of them admit to watching it regularly. Add to this the spectre of progressively depraved rock music and the influence of soak-it-all-up, worldling peers and the picture taking shape strikes terror into the heart of every concerned parent. What can be done?

God has provided every parent with a potent weapon. It is called prayer. *"... The effectual fervent prayer of a righteous man availeth much." (James 5:16).* That's the good news! The bad news is that many parents don't take advantage of it. They watch helplessly as their offspring are gobbled up by the world, the flesh and the devil. They don't realize that the ministry of intercessory prayer is a powerful weapon in the hand of the righteous. They literally *"... have not because [they] ask not." (James 4:2).*

Parents Who Prayed

Unlike these parents, history is replete with the stories of concerned parents who turned to God on behalf of their children. The patriarch Job, fearful of the potential waywardness of his children, continually offered up prayers for them. *"... Job sent and sanctified them, and rose up early in the morning, and offered burnt offerings according to the number of them all: for Job said, It may be that my sons have sinned, and cursed God in their hearts. Thus did Job continually."* *(Job 1:5)* Manoah and his wife, upon learning of the future arrival of baby Samson, cried out, *"... teach us what we shall do unto the child that shall be born!" (Judges 13:8).* What new parent can't identify with them? The father of the child beset by demons in Matthew chapter 17 cried out to Christ, *"Lord, have mercy on my son ..." (vs. 15).* The life-threatening sickness of a newborn baby drove a powerful king to his knees. He wept and cried through the night in fervent fasting and prayer and *"... besought God for the child ..." (2 Samuel 12:16).* In John chapter four a nobleman, worried about his son's fragile health, tracked down Jesus to give Him an urgent plea: *"... Sir, come down ere my child die!" (vs. 49).*

Some people could not be daunted even after death had claimed their children; Jairus in Matthew nine and Elijah in 1 Kings 17 prayed for God to raise up a lifeless child ... and He did!

You Can Have a Ministry of Prayer

Such unction in praying is not limited to the days of the Bible. You, too, can have a life-giving ministry of prayer for your child. Your children certainly need it! They are tender, vulnerable and often defenseless in the face of satanic attacks.

67

Your prayers can shield them from his fiery darts. You can take *"... the shield of faith, wherewith ye shall be able to quench all the fiery darts of the wicked." (Ephesians 6:16)*.

When you plead for your child, you can rest assured that God hears you. *"The eyes of the Lord are upon the righteous, and his ears are open unto their cry." (Psalm 34:15)*. He has an unequaled compassion for the little children. Mark chapter ten records His tender concern for them. *"... he took them up in his arms, put his hands upon them, and blessed them." (vs. 16)*. Their special place in His heart is underscored by dire warnings against mistreating them. *"Take heed that ye despise not one of these little ones;"* Christ warns, *"for I say unto you, That in heaven their angels do always behold the face of my Father which is in heaven." (Matthew 18:10)*.

He makes no bones about the fate of those who "offend" them. *"But whoso shall offend one of these little ones which believe in me, it were better for him that a millstone were hanged about his neck, and that he were drowned in the depth of the sea." (Matthew 18:6)*. The word "offend" used here is from the Greek word "SKANDALIZO" from which we get the word "scandal." Its true meaning is "to cause another to stumble." The picture is that of placing a rock in someone's path to trip them.

To offend a little one is to result in their stumbling in their Christian walk. This may assume the form of an enticement to sin, or some overt offense such as child abuse or molestation.

I wonder how many children have been caused to stumble because of neglect as well? What greater neglect than neglecting to pray for them? *"... God forbid that I should sin against the Lord in ceasing to pray for you..."* (1 Samuel 12:23).

Intercessory Prayer

Intercessory prayer has an impressive legacy. Not only did many of the Bible saints practice it, but Christ Himself was committed to it. His high priestly prayer recorded in John chapter seventeen provides one of the greatest insights into the heart of our Saviour ever recorded. *"I pray for them ... which thou hast given me ... Neither pray I for these alone, but for them also which shall believe on me through their word."* (John 17:9, 20). He not only prayed for His contemporaries, the disciples, but He also prayed for believers living today. Even as you read these words, He is in heaven appealing to God on your behalf; *"For Christ is not entered into the holy places made with hands, which are the figures of the true; but into heaven itself, now to appear in the presence of God for us."* (Hebrews 9:24). This is an eternal ministry! *"... he ever liveth to make intercession ..."* (Hebrews 7:25). Think of it! Christ has been praying for over 2,000 years without interruption!

If this is Christ's passion for us, it should be ours for our children! If this is Christ's priority, it should be ours! If this is Christ's ministry, it should be ours, *"... because as he is, so are we in this world."* (1 John 4:17).

"Scripture Prayer"

Scripture praying is one of the most powerful and effective means of prayer known to man. I stumbled upon this method while praying about my preaching and teaching ministries. I started a prayer list of essential needs I faced in these roles. As I listed these things, specific scriptures came to mind which underscored each need and provided hope for a solution. I applied those scriptures into the very wording of my prayers and made an exciting discovery! I not only experienced more of the things I requested during my preaching, but many people commented on the impact of the message upon their own hearts!

I now have a list of over thirty different, specific requests with attached scriptures, and I pray through the entire list almost without exception each time I preach. It takes approximately one hour to complete this list. That one hour in prayer accomplishes more than ten hours in study!

For example, I know my need to recall the scriptures while preaching, as well as clarity of mind and plainness of speech. While praying for these things one day, my mind was directed to 1 Corinthians 1:5, *"That in every thing ye are enriched by him, in all utterance, and in all knowledge."* I realized that God stands ready to answer this prayer, and He does ... every time! So my prayer for this need goes something like this: "Lord, at my wisest, I am altogether foolish, and my best speech is from lips of clay and a tongue of wood. If you do not help me, this sermon will be an exercise of futility. I ask, therefore, that You would enrich me in all utterance and knowledge." Thus, I pray the Scriptures by making them part of my prayer.

I was surprised and blessed to subsequently learn that this is a common method of prayer for many spiritual saints throughout history. For example, "George Mueller always prayed with an open Bible. He constantly filled his petitions with God's Word. Friends said the orphanage leader would not voice a petition without a 'word from God' to back that petition ... He literally 'prayed' the Word of God."[1]

E.M. Bounds is renown as a fervent prayer warrior and wrote extensively on the subject during his life. He devoted at least four hours a day to prayer, rising regularly at 3 a.m. He, too, discovered the value of using the Scriptures in his prayers. He writes, "The Word of God is the fulcrum (support) upon which the lever of prayer is placed, and by which things are mightily moved. God has committed Himself, His purpose, and His promise to prayer. His Word becomes the basis, the inspiration of our praying, and there are circumstances under which by importunate prayer, we may obtain an addition or an enlargement of His promises."[2]

Charles Spurgeon explains the reason for this power: "Every promise of Scripture is a writing of God, which may be pleaded before Him with this reasonable request, Do as Thou hast said! The Creator will not cheat the creature who depends upon His truth; and far more, the Heavenly Father will not break His Word to His own child."[3]

Richard Burr explains Scripture praying as: "the practice of using God's Word as the foundation of our communion with Him."[4] Eastman expands the thought: "The Word of God is more than a mere foundation for effective praying; it is the actual substance for effective praying."[5]

I would go even further and describe it as a *method* of praying. Within these elements—the foundation of praying, the substance of your prayers and the method of approach to God—the full value of Scripture praying can be seen. This is applying the word of God to your prayers; *"... the word of God, which <u>effectually worketh</u> ... in you that believe" (1 Thessalonians 2:13)* to your prayers.

Scripture praying brings your value system and your priorities into conformity with God and it will always lead you into the will of God. The importance of this cannot be overstated. The goal of prayer is not to get God to conform to your will but to bring your will into conformity to His! It is only then that God hears your prayer. *"... if ye ask any thing according to his will, he heareth us." (1 John 5:14).*

Persistent Prayer

Despite these promises, many parents fail to pray for their children. Why? W. Graham Scroggie, late pastor and Bible scholar suggests an answer: "Such work as this costs. Perhaps unwillingness to pay the price is the reason why so few enter into it."[6] What price is required?

The Apostle Paul tells the Galatian Christians that he *"travails"* over them *"... until Christ be formed in you." (Galatians 4:19).* He wrote of the praying Epaphras of Colosse: *"Epaphras ... saluteth you ... labouring fervently for you in prayers, that ye may stand perfect and complete in all the will of God." (Colossians 4:12).* Scroggie emphasized the cost of real intercessory prayer: "all great movements of the Spirit of God have had their origin in this prayer agony."[7]

Travail, labor, agony — These words imply a resistance to your prayers, something to be overcome. But what exactly is this resistance all about? What resistance does the praying parent face? It is not his own unbelief that is in question here. Nor is it the unwillingness of God to bless him. Rather, it is the enemy himself who is encountered in this struggle. "There are dark and dangerous forces arrayed against the man who would have power with God in prayer" says Scroggie. "...such an one is challenged at every turn."[8] An amazing incident out of the life of Daniel illustrates the reality of this. In chapter ten of his book, he had experienced such a disturbing vision that he could not eat for three full weeks. He poured himself out in mourning and prayer. Afterwards a mysterious messenger appeared unto Daniel to announce that his prayer had been heard on the very first day, but that he had been delayed in bringing the answer from God because of enemy opposition. *"Fear not, Daniel: for from the first day that thou didst set thine heart to understand, and to chasten thyself before thy God, thy words were heard, and I am come for thy words. But the prince of the kingdom of Persia withstood me one and twenty days: but, lo, Michael, one of the chief princes, came to help me; and I remained there with the kings of Persia. Now I am come ..."(10:12-14).*

The "prince" referred to here is none other than Satan himself. It is clear then, that the enemy of our souls will strive to block our prayers. It is with *him* that the striving takes place. "The existence and power of wicked spirits will thus become a very real thing to the intercessor. Today, these facts are, for the most part, denied or ignored, and that is sufficient explanation of our spiritual impotence."[9]

The enemy is never more afraid than when God's people hunker down in serious prayer. He knows there is power in prayer. "We have authority to take from the enemy everything he is holding back. The chief way of taking is by prayer..."[10] This intense type of praying is not only a striving, but a <u>persistent</u> striving. It is repetitious praying. Our Lord prayed three time in the garden *"... saying the same words." (Matthew 26:44).* Twice He prayed for a man's blindness *(Mark 8:23-25).* These are not "vain repetitions," but earnest, soul-felt prayers each time they were uttered.

Eastman contends that Abraham failed in his prayer for the deliverance of Sodom *(Genesis 18:16-33)* because he gave up too soon. Elijah, on the other hand, while praying for rain, prevailed because he pleaded with God seven times *(1 Kings 18:42-45).*[11] Jack Taylor agrees with him. Commenting on these passages, he writes, "Is it without significance that Elijah prayed seven times — the number of perfection and fullness — while Abraham stopped at six times, the number of human frailty?"[12]

Parents tend to get discouraged in prayer. Let's face it, when a child is young and straining at restrictions, it is challenging to maintain faithfulness in prayer, especially if the failures seem to outnumber the victories. That's why Paul encourages us to *"... not be weary in well doing: for in due season we shall reap if we faint not." (Galatians 6:9)*. The victory comes from a commitment to striving and persistence, and few things capture the essence of these things like the ministry of intercessory prayer for your children.

Applied Prayer

How do you use Scripture praying for your children? It is one thing to tell you of the need of Scripture praying, but it is another thing altogether for you to try it yourself. There needs to be a way to incorporate the striving and persistence in your Scripture praying. There is!

I propose a simple 30-day plan which can be used for the lifetime of your child. By identifying the Scriptural priorities you believe God would have for your child and using Scriptures to pray for those needs, you will insure that the most important needs of your child are prayed over regularly. In fact, if you pray for only one need of your child once monthly for twenty years of his lifetime, you will have beseeched God 240 times for that one need! Talk about persistence! This is really *"... effectual, fervent prayer ... [which] availeth much." (James 5:16)*

On these pages, I have outlined a sample approach for

you to follow. You may desire to modify the list to best accommodate the particular needs of your child, but it will give you a pattern to follow. Each month, as you pray these specific Scripture prayers for your child, you will be interceding with God on your child's behalf. May you experience real power in your prayers.

Footnotes:

[1] Eastman, Dick, *The Hour That Changes the World*, Baker, 1998, p. 56.

[2] Taylor, Jack, *Prayer: Life's Limitless Reach,* Broadman, 1977, p. 109.

[3] Bounds, E.M., *The Possibilities of Prayer*, cited in Eastman, p. 56-57.

[4] Burr, Richard, *Developing Your Secret Closet of Prayer,* Christian Publications, 1998, p. 80.

[5] Eastman, p. 57.

[6] Scroggie, W. Graham, *Method in Prayer*, Ambassador, 1997, p. 83.

[7] Ibid.

[8] Ibid., p. 84.

[9] Ibid., p. 84-85.

[10] Harvey, Edwin & Lillian, *Kneeling We Triumph*, Moody, 1974, p. 40.

[11] Eastman, p. 82.

[12] Taylor, P. 75

30 Biblical Virtues to Pray for Your Children

1. **SALVATION** - Lord, I pray that You will bring my child to *"... obtain the salvation which is in Christ Jesus with eternal glory" (2 Timothy 2:10).*

2. **GROWTH IN GRACE** – I pray that my children may *"... grow in grace, and in the knowledge of our Lord and Saviour, Jesus Christ..." (2 Peter 3:18).*

3. **LOVE** – May my children *"... walk in love, as Christ also hath loved us, and hath given himself for us..." (Ephesians 5:2).*

4. **PURITY** – Grant, O God, the grace and strength needed for my child to *"... Keep [himself] pure" (1 Timothy 5:22)* and to *"flee ... youthful lusts..." (2 Timothy 2:22).*

5. **LOVE FOR PARENTS** – God, I pray for love and harmony in our family. I ask especially that You would *"... turn the heart of the fathers to the children, and the heart of the children to their fathers." (Malachi 4:6).*

6. **RESPECT FOR AUTHORITY** – Teach my child to *"... obey [his] parents in the Lord"* and to *"honor [his] father and mother" (Ephesians 6:1-2),* to *"... Honor the King" (1 Peter 2:17)* and all government representatives. Teach him also to *"esteem"* his pastor *"... very highly in love for [his] work's sake" (1 Thessalonians 5:13)* and to be submissive to all spiritual authority whom You choose to place over him.

7. **MERCY**- In this hard-headed and self-centered culture, I pray for my child that he might value the needs of others and the blessings which result from that. You have promised *"Blessed are the merciful, for they shall obtain mercy." (Matthew 5:7)*. I pray that blessing for him.

8. **LOVE FOR GOD'S WORD** – May my children grow to love God's Word and to find it more desirable than *"... much fine gold: sweeter also than honey and the honeycomb." Psalm 19:10.*

9. **LOVE FOR GOD** – Lead my child deeper and deeper into a loving relationship with Thee, Lord. May he *"... love the Lord ... with all [his] heart, and with all [his] soul, and with all [his] mind, and with all [his] strength (Mark 12:30)*. Instill in my children a soul that *"... followeth hard after thee" (Psalm 63:8)* and clings passionately to Thee.

10. **CHOICE OF LIFE MATE** – *"[May] the Lord God of heaven ... send his angel before [my child],"* and direct his paths to Your choice of a mate so we too can say *"... The thing proceedeth from the Lord...the Lord hath spoken" (Genesis 24:7, 50, 51).*

11. **A SERVANT'S HEART** – God, may *"... this mind be in [them] which was also in Christ Jesus ... [who] took upon [himself] the form of a servant..." (Philippians 2:5,7).*

12. **CONTENTMENT** – Teach my children *"... in whatsoever state [they find themselves] therewith to be content." (Philippians 4:11).*

13. **RESISTANCE TO THE DEVIL** – O Lord, give them an awareness of Satan's power without undue fear, and teach them to *"...Resist the devil" (James 4:7)* with the *"...whole armour of God..." (Ephesians 6:13).*

14. BIBLICAL SELF ACCEPTANCE – God, I ask that you lead my children into a deep understanding of who they are in Christ. Help them to see that they are *"accepted in the beloved" (Ephesians 1:6)*, that they are *"... complete in Him" (Colossians 2:10),* and that their *"... sufficiency is of God ..." (2 Corinthians 3:5).*

15. A FORGIVING SPIRIT – Protect my children, O God, from the root of bitterness which troubles so many today. Grant them that they might forgive others *"... even as Christ forgave [them]..." (Colossians 3:13).*

16. WISE CHOICE OF COMPANIONS – Lord, lead my child to choose to *"... [walk] with [the] wise..."* and the wisdom to understand that *"... a companion of fools shall be destroyed..." (Proverbs 13:20).*

17. FEAR OF GOD – Lord, teach my children that *"The fear of the Lord is a fountain of life..." (Proverbs 14:27)* and may he be satisfied (Proverbs 19:23) by drinking of it. Teach him the meaning of this fear and lead him to apply it to his everyday life.

18. FAITH – I pray that a seed of faith, even the size of a *"grain of mustard seed"* may find root in my child's heart *(Luke 17:5-6)*, and move mountains of difficulty.

19. BIBLICAL VIEW OF GOD - May my children see Thee so *"... high and lifted up..." (Isaiah 6:1)* that all else will pale in significance to that vision.

20. HOLINESS – Dear Lord, lead my child's steps that he *"... might be partaker of [thy] holiness..." (Hebrews 12:10).*

21. STRONG WORSHIP LIFE – Teach my children to balance their service with their worship of Thee. Help them to *"... choose that good part which shall not be taken away..." (Luke 10:42).*

22. WISDOM – Lord, *"Wisdom is the principal thing..."* for my children. Help them to get it and in all their *"... getting [help them] get understanding"* as well *(Proverbs 4:7).*

23. CONSISTENT PRAYER LIFE – May my children feel such a kinship with you, O Lord, that they may *"Pray without ceasing." (1 Thessalonians 5:17).*

24. WORK ETHIC – May my children learn that *"In all labour there is profit..." (Proverbs 14:23)* at an early age, and apply themselves to work *"... heartily as to the Lord" (Colossians 3:23).*

25. CHOICE OF CAREER – God, lead the steps of my child to that time and place where *"...it shall be told [him] of all things which are appointed for [him] to do." (Acts 22:10).*

26. GRATITUDE – Create in my child a heart of gratitude that he might *"[give] thanks ... for all things..." (Ephesians 5:20)* and *"... in every thing" (1 Thessalonians 5:18)* for this is the will of God for him.

27. TRUST IN GOD – Dear God, as the Lord Jesus Christ *"... committed himself to him that judgeth righteously" (1 Peter 2:23)* even in His darkest hour, so let my children learn to trust You even in the midst of suffering *(1 Peter 4:19).*

28. JOY – O God, guide them to Your side for *"... in thy presence is fullness of joy..." (Psalm 16:11).* Protect them from dutiful service and may they *"serve the Lord with gladness..." (Psalm 100:2).*

29. HUMILITY – May my child *"Humble [himself] in the sight of the Lord..."* that You might *"... lift [him] up." (James 4:10).*

30. SELF CONTROL – May my children come under the control of the Spirit and enjoy the fruit of *"temperance"* or self control *(Galatians 5:22-23)*.

The king's heart is in the hand of the LORD, as the rivers of water: he turneth it whithersoever he will. (Proverbs 21:1)

Chapter Seven

How to Protect Your Children From Becoming "Gospel Hardened"

A great blessing of founding a Christian school was the frequent comments of visitors about the high level of excitement in the students about spiritual things. Wide-eyed wonderment and genuine excitement over spiritual discoveries abounded. But gradually this was displaced with a growing callousness obvious to all. Fervent students became cynical, guest speakers who had once fawned over the spiritual level of the kids now were silent. The once-excited parents were perplexed, and I was puzzled. How had a spiritually dynamic student body been reduced to a lethargic and cold-hearted group of "I-dare-you-to-change-me" worldlings?

The Bible warns of this phenomenon: *"But exhort one another daily ... lest any of you be hardened through the deceitfulness of sin." (Hebrews 3:13)*. It is a fact of the Christian life that we can be hardened in our hearts to spiritual things. We call this condition "gospel hardening."

The Christian school is a primary target. Worldliness abounds with the latest styles and hairdos as the measure of standing and status. Conversations bristle with references to the latest rock record, last night's TV program, and the upcoming ball game. Conspicuous by its absence is the mention of Christ and the things of God. What has happened? Spiritual deception has set in...our youth are hardened through the "deceitfulness of sin" and don't even know it.

What has brought this blight upon our Christian schools? What is the cause of such coldness? There are several causes, but foremost among them is an American infatuation with the Greek method of learning over the Hebrew method. For example, the Greeks were known for their pursuit of worldly wisdom and their high esteem for the acquisition of knowledge. The Hebrew approach was much more pragmatic and spiritual in its nature. They wanted to see that learning had a godly origin and a positive effect. Given a choice between seeking help from an uneducated but spiritual truck driver with a long-standing and happy marriage and a thrice divorced marriage counselor with a Ph.D. in psychology, the Greek would opt for the Ph.D. Why? Because he has knowledge. The Hebrew would opt for the truck driver. Why? Because he has godliness and a track record to back it up. Like the Greeks before us, we, too, have bowed at the shrine of knowledge.

This approach to learning is most evident in our Bible teaching. Often it reflects a goal of learning facts about the Bible rather than life principles from the Bible. The Bible is treated academically like any other subject, with tests, quizzes and grades. A God-breathed book which is "spirit and life" is reduced to just one more source of knowledge.

Many classes then become a boring but necessary evil in the day's schedule. Gradually our kids become inoculated against the power of truth because they are exposed to an anemic "letter of the law" approach without the "spirit" of it. A vaccination or inoculation is based on a simple premise: the introduction of a small amount of the disease into the body's system stimulates the growth of antibodies to build a resistance against any further full-scaled invasion of the same disease. In a similar way, Christian school students who are vaccinated with small weak doses of the Bible, acquire a dull familiarity with the Scriptures, which desensitizes them to future, life-changing doses of truth. I have seen the youth sections of many churches during the preaching show either a cold disregard for what is said or a disdainful disrespect while they talk and pass notes. Why? They have grown immune to spiritual things. They are gospel hardened.

A dangerous assumption has surfaced in Christianity, most evident in our approach to training. Many feel that just because truth is taught, it will make one spiritual, but this is simply not true. While attending Purdue University, I was amazed to see our English professor bring a Bible to class. For several days he extolled the eloquence and syntax of the King James English and read large portions to the students. Did its presentation make a difference? None that was evident. Why? Because the mere presentation of the truth, though it has some effect, is not the full plan of God for deep change. His plan includes explanation of the truths as well.

The Apostle Paul makes a distinction in the presentation of truth and its explanation. *"...[Y]e have obeyed...,"* he wrote, *"...that form of doctrine which was delivered you." (Romans 6:17).* The "form of doctrine" is the presentation of truth, "delivered you" is the explanation. The difference is significant in the changing of young lives. Imagine yourself at the foot of the cross at the time of the crucifixion. As you listen, you hear several comments about this event. A soldier says, " A man was executed here today." That is the presentation of truth. A Pharisee adds, "A teacher was crucified today." That is the presentation of truth. A woman laments, "A poor, gentle soul was martyred today." That, too, is the presentation of truth. But a disciple explains, "Jesus Christ, the Son of God, died for our sins today." That is the explanation of truth. The presentation of truth without an explanation reduces the Scripture to interesting history or lofty literature. Likewise, when Bible facts are taught out of balance with life principles, they are reduced to cold academics, dead orthodoxy, and a sterile familiarity with holy things. What is needed is an explanation because explanations produce understanding. The Lord Jesus refers to this process as sowing on "good ground." *"But he that received seed into the good ground is he that heareth the word, and understandeth it; which also beareth fruit..." (Matthew 13:23).*

The solution to this dilemma is to engage the heart of the student as well as the mind. Paul wrote to the Roman converts *"...ye have obeyed from the heart..." (Romans 6:17).* The heart is where the facts from the head are processed into action. It is the time when fact becomes faith and knowledge become conviction. It is written about the

Hebrews that their *"...heart made them willing..."(Exodus 35:29)* to give. The Apostle Paul alludes to *"...doing the will of God from the heart." (Ephesians 6:6).*

The question then arises, how is the heart engaged? The Bible gives us clear direction in this matter. Moses instructed his people about the training of their children with inspired words made for our generation. *"And these words, which I command thee this day, shall be in thine heart: And thou shalt teach them diligently unto thy children, and shalt talk of them when thou sittest in thine house, and when thou walkest by the way, and when thou liest down, and when thou risest up." (Deuteronomy 6:6-7).*

In this passage are four vital principles for making the Word of God come alive to the young person.

First in the thoughts of Moses is the **Preparation** of the heart of the teacher: *"...these words...shall be in thine heart." (Deuteronomy 6:6).* The obvious concern of Moses is that the flame of truth in any child's heart should come from the altar of the teacher's heart. It is axiomatic that fire begets fire, and that God's chosen medium to dispense truth is a pure heart. The result of a godly, burning heart is powerful: *"...your zeal hath provoked very many." (2 Corinthians 9:2).* A teacher with such zeal has a tremendous spiritual influence on his students. But the unspiritual teacher must answer the question: *"...how can ye, being evil, speak good things? for out of the abundance of the heart the mouth speaketh." (Matthew 12:34).* If the teacher has fallen prey to the "cares of this world," (aka the athletic program, the academic program, financial pressures, an over-busy schedule, and sin) his own spiritual laxity will certainly be reflected in the coldness of his students. I know of one youth pastor who confessed that, over an eight year period, he never read his Bible except to get a lesson for his teens. It doesn't take a lot of imagination to envision the bankruptcy of such a ministry.

The next principle to which Moses alluded is the principle of **Selection**, specifically the selection of the portion of God's Word which is needed by the listener. The Hebrew word for "teach" is SHANAN, which means "to whet or sharpen." It carries the picture of an archer sharpening his arrow or a butcher his knife. They want to create a point or an edge which will cut and pierce with a specific purpose in mind. Likewise Moses admonishes Israel to sharpen the Word, ignoring irrelevant truth which does not apply to the need at hand, but sharpening the focus of truth to achieve a predetermined purpose. What purpose? To deal with the *"thoughts and intents of the heart."* I have found in my counseling that *"...the word of God is quick, and powerful, and sharper than any twoedged sword, piercing even to the dividing asunder of soul and spirit, and of the joints and marrow, and is a discerner of the thoughts and intents of the heart." (Hebrews 4:12).* When the right portion of the Bible is brought to bear on a specific life problem, the results are amazing. The most powerful use of Scripture is selective use; choosing the precise Scripture for the needs of the listener. As there is a need for information, there is also a need for transformation, and that comes only from specific Scriptures applied to specific needs. Perhaps we need to rethink the coldly systematic approach of Bible training, where the calendar and the clock disallow any divergence from the lesson plan. An approach which includes life-changing truth is needed as well.

It is the life that Moses addressed next. He says that truth should be taught, not merely in a lecture setting, but in the very paths of life where the rubber meets the road; in "the way." This is the principle of **Application.** Application to what? When Moses uses the term, "the way," he is referring specifically to the actions, the behavior, and therefore the lifestyle of the student. Talking with them of the Scriptures "in the way" is in reference to applying the Word of God to life situations as they arise. Walking with a child in the woodlands and observing the birds is a far better time to speak of a God who knows when the sparrow falls than lecturing on it in a windowless room. Likewise, teaching on today's struggles is far better than creating a hypothetical situation not yet encountered. What are our kids thinking about? What are their intents or true purposes in their lives? To ignore these things because of calendar expectations or academic requirements does a disservice to the student. To fail to address them because we haven't taken the time to discern them is negligence.

While pastoring one church, I also was the principal. I invited the senior high students to join me in my study for an informal question and answer time. The major rule was that the Bible was the final authority. In short order the true feelings and doubts of these kids came to the surface. Questions about rock music, sex, dating and even their parents soon found their way into the discussion. I was surprised (shocked?) at the people living under a thin veneer of respectable Christianity. I had entered into the real world of these kids and was privileged to talk with them of the veracity of God's Word as we walked "by the way" together.

I came to realize that what captivated the attention of young people was life principles which addressed their pressing needs and questions. I then tailored a Bible class for juniors and seniors to include a study of temperaments, spiritual gifts, dating and marriage preparation. They absolutely came alive! The Bible was real to them now, and they listened with new attentiveness and wrote with insights which belied their age! I believe that our young people are intelligent and inquisitive. In their youthful idealism, they need answers for living. With a little imagination and effort our Bible classes can be transformed from tombs of the dead into laboratories of the living.

That brings us to the final principle of Moses' instruction; the principle of **Conversation.** The word "talk" in Deuteronomy 6 is a multi-dimensional word translated 85 different ways in the King James Bible. Its meanings include: to declare, converse, command, promise, warn and even sing. It has the meaning of a conversational interchange around the things of God. As the teacher and student walk along the way, they discuss the Word of God and its applications to life. This provides the wise teacher with the opportunity to learn the doubts, fears, confusion and even lack of understanding of his pupils, so that he can correct these with the truth of God.

There are specific ways this can be accomplished in the Bible class. For example, pressing social issues could be assigned as a topic for an essay with the requirement that pre-assigned Scriptures be the sole authority. After the writing, these topics could be discussed as a group with a wise teacher guiding the students to form their conclusions from the Bible. Subjects like divorce, abortion, euthanasia, rock music, drugs, the lottery, forms of entertainment, etc. would grip the imagination because of their high profile in our culture.

Classes on current events would be exciting as the kids see how these things relate to Scriptures. Other meaningful ways to reach the heart with the Scriptures would be inter-class debate teams or field trips to local missions or missionary works, not only to see the need of humanity, but also to make sin become *"... exceedingly sinful." (Romans 7:13).* Video presentations to spark discussion, and plays and skits to illustrate biblical truths in the lives of Bible characters are also effective. The chapel platform should be kept hot and targeted on the needs of the kids.

Another way of exhorting daily is to assign counselors for one-on-one discipleship, counseling, and prayer with each individual student. Faculty and staff could be enlisted for such service, as could church members, parents and other volunteers. Grandparents would be a special pool for such a ministry. Such special attention would provide loving care, special attention, godly direction and needed accountability.

What an avenue for ministry for those looking for involvement in God's service!

Don't misunderstand the intentions of these musings. I am not suggesting that the baby be thrown out with the bath water. I am not advocating that all Bible curriculums be dumped! At the very least, they should be enhanced and supplemented enough to keep life issues in front of the kids while teaching them factual information.

Moses stresses principles of teaching which included the preparation of the teacher, the careful selection of Scriptures, application of those truths to real-life situations, and the inclusion of conversation between the student and teacher. The children of Israel had great advantages through these principles. Do our kids deserve any less?

Chapter Eight

Sour Grapes

"What mean ye, that ye use this proverb concerning the land of Israel, saying, The fathers have eaten sour grapes, and the children's teeth are set on edge?" -Ezekiel 18:2

There is much confusion among Christians today about the role of leadership in the lives of young people. Some say the parent is solely responsible for the outcome of the child, while others insist that it's the child himself, who really is responsible for his decisions, his direction, and even his destiny.

This question hangs on the horns of a major dilemma. The Bible seems to teach more than one thing on this subject. On the one hand, Solomon makes it clear (?) that the responsibility rests solely on the parents; *"Train up a child in the way he should go, and when he is old, he will not depart from it."(Proverbs 22:6)*. This seems like an airtight argument until you apply the analogy of faith to it and compare scripture with scripture. For example, the Apostle Paul argues for the individual's responsibility rather than the parent's; *"So then every one of us shall give account of himself to God."(Romans 14:12)*.

It seems confusing at best to say on the one hand that the responsible for the child's decisions and actions belongs to the parent, and on the other hand that the responsibility is to be placed on the head of the child. Indeed, surrounding the issue of child training is a storm of confusion, misunderstanding, and controversy. At the eye of the storm is the central issue concerning every parent of a child; who _is_ responsible for the finished product?

A large reason for this confusion is an insidious philosophy called "determinism." The heart of this belief is that man is the product of factors beyond his control; his character, personality and even his spirituality have been "determined" by these factors beforehand, and he is therefore the victim and/or product of his past, his parents, his culture, and psychological influences, This is the theory embraced by the Jews of the Old Testament. They firmly held that the behavior of the children is simply a reaction to the parents' action.

This belief was later popularized by that arch enemy of the cross, Sigmund Freud. It was one of the planks in the perverted platform of his theory of psychodynamics which includes such stellar beliefs as the id, the ego, the subconscious, and the Oedipus complex (which insisted that every child grew up jealous of and hating the parent of the same sex and wanting to kill them because of a morbid jealousy borne out of his love for the parent of the opposite sex.) And this noble belief is justified by Freud in large measure because that's how _he_ felt.

Freud's initial contribution to this area of determinism was focused on psychological determinism; an attempt to remove guilt by placing it at the door of an offending parent, After all my mother slapped me when I was two and bruised my id, Therefore it's not my fault I'm the way I am but my mother's.

There is a truism which says, "What one generation does in moderation, the next will do in excess." Predictably, succeeding generations took Freud's initial hypothesis of psychic determinism to excess. Today we have racial determinism, birth order determinism, environmental determinism, economic determinism, genetic determinism, chemical determinism, biological determinism, etc., and the one most in question before us, parental determinism.

If this belief had been limited to the world, it would have been one thing; but for the church to embrace it as well is quite another. And there seems to be an identifiable time in history when this occurred. When Freud's teaching on this subject appeared in print at the very beginning of the twentieth century, a famous preacher of the day praised it as the answer for many problems. It is coincidental that this was about the same time that it became fashionable to preach Proverbs 22:6 as the proof text for Freudian determinism; after all, it seemed to fit.

Was Freud a man used by sinister forces to spoil the church? It would seem so. "Beware lest any man spoil you through philosophy and vain deceit, after the tradition of men, after the rudiments of the world, and not after

Christ." (Colossians 2:8). He certainly used philosophy based on the Jewish tradition of men, as he was Jewish himself; and he seemed hell-bent on spoiling Christianity since the day he observed Christians mistreat his father on the streets of Vienna, Austria and vowed revenge on Christianity. If ever a man got revenge on Christianity by spoiling her, it was Freud.

Largely through his influence, determinism quickly gained a foothold in the Church; at first with only a crack in the door, but later taking command of the pulpit itself. This is seen in three primary areas: the philosophy of church success since, after all, it is believed that everything rises and falls on leadership, personal adult responsibility, since adult Christians blame the parents of their childhood, and child rearing practices, since current parents and their children have been taught that good children are the result of good training and bad children the result of bad parenting.

Once the church was conquered, the sanctity of the home was invaded. We were told that dysfunctional homes produced victimized children who merely reflect the parenting they received. Therefore, any sinfulness on the part of the child is the responsibility of the parent.

I recall that as a young pastor and new parent, I preached often on this power of parents to produce a spiritual giant. It never occurred to me as I thundered from the pulpit on the parent's responsibilities that the children were listening; in fact, they were all ears! Even teenagers who normally weren't tuned in sat bolt upright, glued to every word! And so they should! I was basically telling them that their sin was their parents' fault, a teaching they were altogether eager to embrace. (They were less eager, it seems, to embrace the mirror truth that their success must be their parent's victory, In fact, most deterministic teaching seems to focus more on shifting the blame than sharing the credit, a worthwhile thought to ponder.) Like many sincere but misguided lawmakers of our day who adopt laws intending to do good, and instead make matters worse, I had, in an attempt to put the fear of God in the parents, removed it from the children.

Have you ever noticed that there's no greater expert on child rearing than those "what ain't got none?" that there's no greater expert on rearing teens than parents with small children? and no greater expert on dealing with adult children than parents with teens? It seems we are most authoritative in areas we have the least experience. If you really want help in rearing your children, ask the unmarried family member his advice at the next family gathering. (On the other hand, you may not have to ask!) And I certainly fell prey to this pattern; here I was a young preacher with a young child expostulating on the need of Freudian determinism with a holy zeal and evangelistic fervor.

But all this notwithstanding, the responsibility for a child's behavior took a dramatic shift and then began bouncing around the walls of the church and home like a marble in an out-of-control pin ball machine; the church blames the parents, the parents blame the church, both blame the school, the Christian school blames the world, the world blames society, society blames the government, the government blames the media, the media blames the consumer, but nobody blames the child!

Even a famous Christian psychologist fell prey to this blame-shifting tendency as he recalled a memorable event from his childhood. He had hurt a Sunday School classmate by mockingly referring to his large ears as "jeep fenders." Years later in writing about this, it never occurred to him to take responsibility for his actions: "Looking back on the episode," he writes, "I hold my teachers responsible for that event. They should have told me what it feels like to be laughed at." This conclusion would be laughable if it did not come from the most influential Christian psychologist of our time, who is constantly quoted as an authority.

Mothers are not exempt from these attacks either. In 125 articles surveyed, researchers found 72 psychopathologies in children which were allegedly caused by their mothers! Talk about leaving the blame at the flap of the parent's tent.

And can I ever forget that memorable morning when I awoke to my clock radio blaring out a song by Hank Williams Jr., "Don't ask me 'Hank, why do you drink? Why do you roll smoke? Why do you live by the songs that you wrote?' Put yourself in my position and then you'll know it's a family tradition." Even Hank Jr, blames Hank Sr, for his hang-ups! The Christian is not the only one to embrace determinism.

The victim mentality has taken over our culture. There is a concerted effort by society to shift all responsibility away from the individual to the forces in his life which "determined" (or better yet, "predetermined") him to be the way he is. This is the stock in trade emphasis of the TV talk shows, pop psychology, politically correct self-esteem teachings, and humanistic psychiatry. It seems that Christian teachings which have grown out of a misapplication of Proverbs 22:6 align themselves much more closely with the thinking of the world than the Word of God. Ignoring the clear teachings of Scriptures such as Ezekiel chapter eighteen, which proves that any generation can offset the influence of their parenting, whether good or bad, many seem determined to parrot the philosophy of the world.

We have believed the lie of determinism! More than that, we have practiced it and even promoted it – all this to our shame and our children's harm! It is time to examine this crucial issue and confront the troubling question; Who is responsible for a child's destiny? We need to re-think the popular theory that good training is the sole cause of good behavior, and bad training is the primary culprit for producing bad kids; a belief founded on the philosophy of "sour grapes" in Ezekiel chapter eighteen.

Chapter Nine

Sour Grapes Have a Lousy Aftertaste

Considering the Consequences of Determinism

In Ezekiel chapter eighteen, one of the most amazing writings ever penned about parents and their children, God devastates the common argument that parents bear the iniquity of the children. In no uncertain terms, He takes the Jewish people to task for perverting His Word for their own purposes. To facilitate their sinful embracing of this false belief, they had formed it into a proverb which rolled off their tongues with a well-oiled ease born of much usage; "The fathers have eaten sour grapes, and the children's teeth are set on edge." (Ezekiel 18:2).

God addresses the same deterministic belief in the thinking of the Jewish people that is popular today. They had codified it into a proverb they were fond of quoting in order to blame their parents and justify themselves.

In other words, they claimed that they were not to blame for their sins, but were merely reflect their parenting. The parents acted, they as children reacted. The parents ate sour grapes, the children's teeth were set on edge. Therefore they could not be held responsible; it was their parent's fault. Sound familiar? It should. This is modern day psychology in ancient garb. These Israelites were justifying their sinful behavior in the same way that modern man does today, by blaming their parents.

God's response was immediate; "What mean ye, that ye use this proverb concerning the Land of Israel...? This was a question not in response to a one-time use of the proverb but to a longtime, chronic practice. An otherwise patient God seems to have reached a turning point;"As I live, saith the Lord God, ye shall not have occasion any more to use this proverb in Israel." (vs. 3). Then with one piercing stroke of the sword, He exposes the thoughts and intents of their hearts; "Behold, all souls are mine; as the soul of the father, so also the soul of the son is mine: the soul that sinneth, it shall die."(vs. 4).

The ultimate cause of sin is a low view of God, and the predictable result of sin is a further distortion of the doctrine of God. In their misconception of God's sovereignty, they dishonored God and perpetuated this dishonor in all who agreed with them. This view is reflected in God's rebuke above. He reminds them of an obvious truth they had rejected; God is owner of every soul, and every soul is answerable directly to Him.

But the Israelites' response to God's rebuke was to attack God Himself; "Yet ye say, The way of the Lord is not equal [just] ..." (vs. 25).

Ultimately, their thinking followed the predictable course of lowering God to elevate man, a path still followed by many today. Their thinking had become so deeply affected by their wrong beliefs that now they saw God as unfair for even suggesting that they were responsible for their own actions. They reasoned thusly; "If sin is hereditary, my response is merely reactionary. Now, God, if you punish me for my parent's sins, You're arbitrary!" And quite frankly, if they were right about the cause of their sin, they would have a valid point. This is precisely why children today question the goodness of God who convicts them and disciplines them for actions that they, for the life of themselves, cannot see as their fault. Scriptural truth has a difficult time penetrating this formidable defense. But not only is the doctrine of God called into question by this belief, so is the doctrine of parenting.

They were absolutely convinced that they had to bear the iniquity of their fathers which translates into dying because of their fathers' sins. (See vs. 19 compared to vs. 17.) This resulted in a despairing fatalism which convinced them that they were not only doomed to live a sinful life like their fathers, but that they had no recourse but to go to the grave in the helpless grip of their sin. How many people today believe that because their parents were alcoholics, they, too, will be; because a parent committed suicide, they will also; because their parents had chronic sin patterns in their lives, they would as well; and not only would they have it, they would take it to the grave. How awful to have this view of parenting; that the parents are to blame for my sin, that I am the way I am because of their failure and nothing can change that! And how wrong this is!

I grew up in the home of a Baptist preacher. My father founded and pastored the Miller Road Baptist Church in Garland, Texas after graduating from Dallas Theological Seminary. He was a committed student of the Word, comfortable in the Greek and Hebrew languages, and wrote books which are beyond my comprehension. Nevertheless, as a young teenager, I concluded in my imminent wisdom that he was woefully ignorant, and took it upon myself to leave home. So, at age sixteen, I packed my bags, took his car and set out to make a life for myself determined that nobody was going to tell me what to do. I then enrolled in Bob Jones Academy in Greenville, SC where they told me what I could not do, but even told me what I should do. I left home out of anger but the anger never left me. I had swallowed the theory of determinism hook, line, and sinker! I believed that my Dad was to blame for all my problems.

So one day in my imagination (and I have been told it's an active one), I decided to ask my Dad a question that had been bothering me for some time. I went to him in my mind with a microphone to do a man-on-the-street type interview, thrust the mike into his face, and intoned in my most professional journalistic voice, "Dad, why were you such a bad dad to me to give me all these hang-ups?" I just knew that this would stop him cold in his tracks. He never missed a beat; "Why Jimmy," he replied. "It's not my fault; it was the way I was brought up." In other words, he was saying that it wasn't his fault, it was Grandpaw's. (It rarely occurs to the determinist that if they have the right to blame their parents, their parents have the right to blame theirs.) So

I went to Grandpaw. "Grandpaw, why were you such a bad dad to my dad to give him hang-ups which caused him to be a bad dad to me and give me hang-ups!?" "Jimmy," he said. "It's not my fault, it's the way I was brought up." Well, you can see where this is taking us can't you? All the way back to the Garden. And guess what Adam said, "It ain't my fault! It's the woman you gave me!" And guess what Eve said, "It ain't my fault. It's the snake's!" And he didn't have a leg to stand on.

And neither do we! The logical end of this illogical thinking is that ultimately nobody is to blame, nobody that is but God. Matthew Henry makes it clear what the intent of the Jews were; he maintains that this proverb "thus charges Him with injustice ... They intended it as a reflection on, and an impeachment of His equity." How unfair to give me such parents! We complain. How unjust to expect me to ever rise above my heritage! How cruel to punish me for sins which were forced upon me by my parents!

The result of this of course is a careless and deceitful mishandling of the Word which removes personal choice from the table. After all, if I am merely the product of parenting, if I merely react to mom and dad's sin, I can't help sinning. It's not my fault. I have no choice in the matter.

This is why it is so important to apply an important rule of Bible interpretation called the analogy of faith **1.**. Before making a determination on any teaching of the Bible, I must compare the text before me to all the texts around the truth of this text. When we apply Romans 6:16 to the truth of determinism for example, the insistence that we have no choice is called into question to say the least; "Know ye not, that to whom ye yield yourselves servants to obey, his servants ye are to whom ye obey; whether of sin unto death, or of obedience unto righteousness?"

The Apostle Paul asks a sobering question here; "Do you not realize that you can choose to be a slave to sin or to righteousness? And that ultimately, your choice determines which master you follow?" Wow! Talk about a silver bullet! No child is doomed to follow his parents' sinfulness or destined to follow their righteousness. He is a free moral agent with all the powers of personal choice.

To believe otherwise as the Jews did, is to remove yourself from the truth of God which brings guilt and conviction of sin. After all, how can you be convicted of your sin when nothing is your fault? If each time that God speaks to you of your sin you deflect the responsibility onto your parents, how are you to ever be convinced of your role? If no truth, then, no conviction, if no conviction, no repentance, if no repentance, no confession, if no confession, no forgiveness, if no forgiveness, no hope! And there in microcosm is the picture of the church today. So many pew sitters are so bitter at their parents, so hardened in their belief their helpless state was imposed on them by unfair parenting, and so convinced that it's not their fault, that they can't get the victory they so desire. Where is the hope in that!? It is to face the truth which God is making so clear; each one of us is responsible for his sin!

This Jewish line of thinking has dragged a dark cloud of confusion over a very clear sky in Christian living. People by the score claim to be infected by their parents' sin while their parents oblige them by deflecting any guilt which God brings upon their offspring. Like an umbrella in a rainstorm, they spread their parental responsibility over the head of their young lest any drop of Spirit-sent conviction settle on them.

I recall vividly preaching on this subject in California when afterwards a weeping mother dragged her less than enthusiastic son down the aisle with her to talk with me. As she wept and bemoaned her failure as a mother, the son, who was not at all happy to share in this moment, caught my attention. His ball cap was on backwards, scraggly hair peeked out from under its rim barely hiding the fuzz on his unshaven cheeks. His pant cuffs flopped loosely over his shoes while the pants hung almost to his knees. (fortunately his shirt hung below them). His t-shirt blared forth some unmentionable expletive which framed a bloody skull. He had metal in every loose flap of skin from his shoulders upward; eyebrows, nose, ears, and tongue. His mother tearfully bemoaned her failure; "Where did I go wrong? I tried to raise him right. I took him to church, read him the Bible and prayed with him, but now he's on drugs and runs around with the worst kids imaginable. He's flunking in school and faces a court hearing. Where did I go wrong!?" In the meantime, the boy is leaning against the end of a pew with folded arms, rolling eyes, and a look of sullen disdain, as if to say, "Will you tell the old lady where she went wrong so I can get out of here!? " I thought to myself, "What's wrong with this picture?" Here is a son living in sin to whom God is trying to grip with the strong hand of His conviction. The mother, in essence, had reached over, grabbed the hand and removed it from her son's head and placed it on her own. So the son, who needs guilt, has none and the mother, who deserves little, has it all. She had no idea how she hardened that boy in his rebellion, while he was clueless about his own responsibility.

She was infected with a guilt which said, I am guilty because of my son's sins while any guilt he should have had was deflected with the assurance that he was not to blame ... this was Mom's fault. He was blocked from conviction and detoured from repentance because of a misguided mother's deterministic beliefs. More confusion.

And the ultimate tragedy in this thinking is its effect upon hope. What hope did these Israelites have for themselves, for their children? If their righteousness and happiness depended upon sinful parents, they had none. If their children's righteousness and happiness depended upon their holiness, they had none. The black cloud thickens.

I remember reading a famous Christian psychiatrist who said that 85 per cent of a child's personality is formed by age six. This warning was meant to motivate the parent of the toddler to devote themselves to that child while there was hope. I felt sorry for any parents of the seven year old; "Oh dear, I've got only 15 per cent to work with for the rest of my life"! This is a classic example of teaching truth out of balance. While true that there is hope for the young and it is important to *"Chasten thy son while there is hope ..." (Proverbs 19:18),* it is not to say that this is the only time for hope. This would do a great disservice to the promises of salvation and the power of God to forgive sin. Childhood is a time to maximize your influence as a parent. Clearly the little child is of a soft heart and a teachable spirit more than at any other time.

But any Bible student knows that God can radically transform the most hardened criminal at the point of salvation. *"Therefore if any man be in Christ, he is a new creature: old things are passed away; behold, all things are become new." (2 Corinthians 5:17).*

Who can forget the infamous Son of Sam killer who terrorized an entire city for months? Sentenced for his crimes, he later became horrified at what he had done. After some time in prison, he repented of his sins and put his trust and faith in Christ's shed blood as the total payment for his sins. He became a "new creature". Now this once calloused killer is a soft-hearted and meek believer who has devoted the rest of his life to ministering for Christ, even though behind bars. He sees this as his appointed place of service and strives to make his life count for eternity.

No matter what the monsters of the past, any sinner can overcome them with the powerful arsenal of spiritual weapons given him at the moment of salvation: a Bible to instruct him, the Holy Spirit to empower him, prayer to connect him to God, a pastor to shepherd him, a church to support him, the blood of Christ to regularly cleanse him, etc.

God has made every provision for the soul's watchcare, and that is where the parent's faith should be; in God!

God is not limited to the time of salvation, however. He can turn a Christian's life on its head and revive the most hardened at will. *"The king's heart is in the hand of the Lord, as the rivers of water: he turneth it whithersoever he will." (Proverbs 21:1).*

To fail to believe in this power, never to embrace this hope, is to experience ultimate fatalism. And thus today, I hear adults say, "I can't change!" And young people assert, "I don't have to change."

The church joins the world in lockstep formation while marching to the drumbeat of Freud and acquiring the vocabulary of the hopeless. It's not fear, it's a "phobic disorder" like "agoraphobia," "anxiety disorder," "panic disorder," or "obsessive compulsive disorder." We no longer have lust but "impulse control disorder." It's not rebellion but "oppositional defiant disorder," not sin but "dysfunction" or a "self-biased impulse drive." It seems that we have a "disorder" for many things we once called sin.

How is one to come under conviction if he's a victim rather than a sinner?! We have dissimulated, prevaricated, denied, justified, shifted the blame, and bobbed and weaved so skillfully that the hand of God's conviction can't seem to find us.

If He touches us at all, we convince ourselves that what we're feeling is the residual effect of our parents' sins clinging to us and making us miserable; ascribing their

110

influence to a psychologized vocabulary. We adopt words like sexual misconduct for rape, sexually active for fornication, infidelity for adultery, disease for drunkenness, success motivation for greed, pro-choice for murder, self esteem for self centeredness, misstatement for lie, mistake for sin, and love for lust.

Until we stop justifying our sin by the language of the world and start judging our sin by the language of the Word, we will never have revival in our hearts or in our homes. And until we refuse to let the world define the terms, the cause, and the treatment of sinful behaviors, we will never enjoy victory.

Parents, your child needs to hear the truth in love and you need to come back to a raw-boned, never-say-die faith in the power of God to change the human heart. The very scope of a frustrated search for help from psychology rather than a committed life of prayer is an indication that we have lost something precious; we are looking to replace the power of God or to at least supplement it. Christian psychology itself has admitted its lack of faith in the sufficiency of God's Word. When it insists on adding the wisdom of men to it via an innocuous sounding compromise like "integrated counseling," (a practice which insists that the most effective counseling is the application of man's wisdom mixed, or integrated with God's wisdom), it concedes to a failure of God's Word.

Indeed, sour grapes have a lousy aftertaste; the doctrines of God, of parenting, and of personal choice are distorted beyond measure. A cloud of confusion has blanketed the Christian world and the home. We no longer have clarity regarding personal guilt, sin, and above all, hope. We have witnessed a gross deterioration in the thinking of our age when sin is no longer sin and is justified by the language of the world. Why has this happened? How have we come to such a place?

Note: "The Analogy of Faith" in Bible interpretation:

Defined: "The constant and perpetual harmony of Scripture in the fundamental points of faith and practice deduced from those passages in which they were discussed by the inspired penmen either directly or expressly, and in clear, plain, and intelligible language."

The basic assumption here is that there is one system of truth or theology contained in Scripture, and therefore all doctrines must cohere or agree with each other. That means that the interpretations of specific passages must not contradict the total teaching of Scripture on a point. This is similar to saying that Scripture interprets Scripture. (emphasis added)

From: Protestant Biblical Interpretation, p. 107
by Bernard Ram, Baker Book House, 1970

Chapter Ten

If Sour Grapes Taste So Bad, Why Do We Keep Eating Them?

The Causes of Determinism

If sour grapes taste so bad, why do we keep eating them? In short, we have taught philosophy as theology, we have substituted a general principle for an absolute promise, and we have confused an influence with a cause. Let me explain.

Teaching Philosophy as Theology

It has always been the goal of the deceiver, and his method of choice, to call evil good. He loves to elevate baser things to the higher ground of moral advantage. For example, what better way to lead the naïve into sin than by calling lust "love"? He has not only made it more appealing for young lovers to fornicate but almost an expected expression of their love.

It is equally effective to elevate sin to the level of a "disorder," to justify evil by labeling it a "mental illness," to eliminate the stigma of drunkenness by calling it a "disease," etc.

And the most coveted high ground for the father of lies is the vaunted mountain peak of theological truth. Now the issue is not only morally appealing but God-endorsed! As a theology, it can be preached from the pulpit and practiced in the pew with abandon. So dangerous is this tendency, that God screams a warning to us from the pages of Scripture; "Beware lest any man spoil you through philosophy and vain deceit, after the tradition of men, after the rudiments of the world, and not after Christ." (Colossians 2:8). Unfortunately, many fail to see the warning and embrace the philosophy wrapped in the pristine garb of theology. Why?

Determinism is a ready-made and easily dispensed means of justifying sin. If my teeth are set on edge because my father ate sour grapes, what more do I need? The sinner can now have his cake and eat it too. If he loathes to part with his sin, he doesn't have to. If he wants to keep his sin and also enjoy the benefits of religion, he can do that too, with no pangs of conscience to interfere with his reverie. In fact, even if he's faced with a choice of forsaking his sin, he knows he can't succeed so why try. It was a similar option which faced the Jewish nation at one point of their history and became the ground zero of their drift from God.

Exodus chapter twenty records this momentous point of time when determinism seems to have gotten its birth. God is presenting the Ten Commandments to Israel and comes to the commandment forbidding idolatry;"Thou shalt not make unto thee any graven image, or any likeness of any thing that is in heaven above, or that is in the earth beneath,

114

or that is in the water under the earth. Thou shalt not bow down thyself to them, nor serve them: for I the Lord thy God am a jealous God, visiting the iniquity of the fathers upon the children unto the third and fourth generation of them that hate me; And showing mercy unto thousands of them that love me, and keep my commandments." (Exodus 20:4-6).

Without a doubt, God is seeking to motivate the Jews to holiness. He has given them clear consequences of their sin and generous blessings for their righteousness. There is judgment to avoid and responsibility to embrace.   These revolve around their children and grandchildren to the third and fourth generation. The warning centers on the fallout effect of their sinfulness upon future generations. After all, if a parent burns down his own home, he children will suffer as homeless. And if the parent worships a false god, the judgment inflicted on them will of necessity be shared by the children.

This is in reference to the nature of sin and not to the nature of the children. The nature of sin is to rain affliction and harm on those in proximity to the sinner targeted by the rainstorm. The New Testament teaches that if a man be troubled by sin, *"thereby many be defiled." (Hebrews 12:15).*

This scripture teaches this very thing. It is not saying that the nature of the children will be permanently cast in the mold of the parents. The Jews were not told that they were entering upon an unbreakable pattern of unavoidable sinfulness. At any point, any generation could change the practice of the previous generation's sin. What a gracious God! Rather, they were warned that the consequences of their sin would be experienced by future generations.

At the same time, one can only marvel at the contrast between God's judgment and His blessing; on the one hand God threatens only two or three generations with the fallout of the parents' sins, but on the other hand promises mercy to thousands of generations for the righteousness of the parents. How lopsided is that!? It's like saying to your children; "Now look honey, if you hit your sister, I'll have to slap your wrist. But if you refrain, I'll take you to Disney World"! What normal, reasonable person faced with such widely opposite options wouldn't choose the greater one?

The answer is the one who wants his sin and sees a way of having it with total justification. At some point, some wicked Israelites saw their chance; they remembered this warning of God and saw a proof text for their sin. They had a biblical basis for blaming their parents. A philosophy became theology. This ultimately became so ingrained in Jewish thinking, they codified it into a permanent proverb;"The fathers have eaten sour grapes and the children's teeth are set on edge."

This is not to say that a sinful parent will not have a negative impact on his children or that a righteous parent cannot have a positive effect. After all, a child reared in home A where God is worshiped, the Bible taught, family prayers are practiced, sin is avoided, church is attended, and salvation enjoyed will have a great advantage over a child reared in home B where sinfulness abounds. But because he is brought up in a good home does not mean he can't go bad. That is the very argument of Ezekiel 18:5-13. A wicked son can come out of a godly home.

On the other hand, because a child is reared in an ungodly home does not mean he can't be righteous. That is the argument of Ezekiel 18:10-17. The theory of sociologists today is that the child of such a home is destined to repeat the sins to which he's been exposed. Brought up in a home where he is molested, abandoned, abused, ignored, or hated, the impact seems initially overwhelming, but not permanently. The negative effect of such a home has clear limitations.

It is limited in its intensity. *"There hath no temptation taken you but such as is common to man: but God is faithful, who will not suffer you to be tempted above that ye are able; but will with the temptation also make a way to escape, that ye may be able to bear it." (1 Corinthians 10:13).* What a hope-saturated truth! What a faith-building scripture! There is no temptation from our past, nothing in our present or even the future which is so strong that it can't be escaped! God is too faithful to not provide that way!

It is limited in duration. *"... if any man be in Christ, he is a new creature: old things are passed away; behold, all things are become new." (2 Corinthians 5:17).* The bondage of sin can never exceed the long arm of grace; *"...where sin abounded, grace did much more abound" (Romans 5:20).* Whether for you or your child, realize that the effects of childhood are limited and God's grace is unlimited and abounding!

And never forget, its limited in finality. Sin does not have the final answer. You are not locked into an inescapable pattern inherited from your parents. You can break the chains of learned repetitive wickedness in your family tree by choosing to love God. *"And shewing mercy unto thousands of them that love me, and keep my commandments." (Exodus 20:6).*

You have the power to usher in the mercies and blessings of God as a direct result of your decision to follow God. This is the truth presented in Ezekiel 18:14-17. Here is a young man who grew up as an eye witness to all his father's sins. These included robbery, murder, and adultery to name a few. This boy was there! He saw his father doing these unthinkable things! Most psychological experts would not give that boy much of a chance of having a normal life let alone a spiritual one. And yet, in an amazing rebuttal of such thinking, God says that the boy *"...seeth all his father's sins which he hath done, and considereth, and doeth not such like"! (vs. 14)* [emphasis added]. The next few verses reveal that this boy grew up to become a godly and righteous man!

Nobody's family tree is fully written. Even the roots and branches of the past are history and not prophecy. The ultimate limbs and leaves of the future are not yet determined because at every generation, another choice is made. What choice are you making?

Equating a General Principle with an Absolute Promise

Is Proverbs 22:6 a general principle or an absolute promise? What is the meaning of this verse? *"Train up a child in the way he should go: and when he is old, he will not depart from it."*

Some believe that this verse teaches that if you train them right, they will turn out right and do right. Conversely if they're doing wrong, it's because they were trained incorrectly.

Others assert that the training here is related to the "bent" of the child. Every child is unique and must be approached according to their unique personality. In other words, you don't tell an outgoing child that children are to be seen and not heard, nor do you force a shy child to stand on the picnic table at the family reunion and sing a solo. Rather, you guide them in the path of their unique temperament, you train theme in the sphere of their propensities. In this way, it is assumed, you maximize the positive effect of training.

Another view is that if trained correctly, the child may go astray; but because of the good training, he will return. This admittedly is a stretch and hard to find in the passage. Nonetheless it is taught, probably by the parent of a teenager.

A unique view is one which asserts that this isn't a promise but a warning. If you train your children in the way he wants to go, if you let him do what he wants to do, when he is old, he will be so entrenched in his evil, he will never turn from it.

119

The common denominator of all these views is determinism. Each of them are saying that the training determines the outcome, and that the parent is ultimately responsible for the child's destiny. They believe strongly that Proverbs 22:6 is an ironclad promise to be claimed.

Although some of the Proverbs are promises, others are not. For example, consider Proverbs 15:1; *"A soft answer turneth away wrath..."*. If you believe that is a promise, take it to the ghetto. When a man points a gun at you and growls, "Your money or your life"! You may think to yourself; "Hmmm, 'a soft answer turneth away wrath', and say, "Aww, you've had a bad day haven't you? I'm so sorry. Do you want to talk about it"? After you pick yourself up off the sidewalk, if you're able, you must conclude; "It's all my fault. I didn't have a soft enough answer". This is what society in general is concluding. It's our fault. We cause the crime in our streets. It has become so popular to blame parents for the child's misbehavior that the courts have gotten involved; parents are being fined and punished for their children's indiscretions; and in one remarkable instance, a woman took her parents to court for letting her be born, contending that if she had not been, she wouldn't have so many problems.

On the other hand, you may conclude, "God lied to me. I had a soft answer and it didn't work." These two conclusions are being believed by Christian parents by the thousands; it's all my fault and/or God lied to me. And both conclusions are based on the distortion of deterministic thinking.

The obvious solution is to see this as a general principle, not an absolute promise. Generally speaking, a soft answer will turn away wrath, but every time? It's akin to the saying, "Get a college education and you will find a good job" or "Don't play in the street or you'll get hit by a car." Generally speaking these statements are true, but to view them as a promise can set you up.

There are some very compelling reasons to conclude that this verse teaches a   general principle rather than an absolute promise. On the negative side, some bad kids have come from a good environment. Consider the second generation in Ezekiel 18. Verses 5-13 show a boy reared by a very godly father but who turned out to be bad. Adam and Eve were brought up in a perfect and sinless environment and still sinned. Whose fault was that? The prodigal son had a godly father (a picture of God the Father) and yet ended up in the pig pen. Even the nation Israel, with the best of all parents, sinned, causing God to rebuke them; *"...the Lord hath spoken, I have nourished and brought up children, and they have rebelled against me." (Isaiah 1:2).* It is unthinkable that God would expect more of your children that His own children could deliver.

On a positive note, God wants us to know that good kids can come from a bad environment. (Ezekiel 18:10-17). Let's face it; here is a father who deserves a permanent niche in the criminal's hall of fame. Not only was he a chronic idolater, and a cruel manipulator of the poor for his own benefit, he was also a man who criminally squeezed interest from unsuspecting borrowers to make more money at their expense. In addition, he was a chronic adulterer, violent in his actions against others, a committed thief, and thought nothing of murdering the innocent. And yet from the home of this father, a godly son arose!

When comparing scripture with scripture, one is forced to conclude that not only does man have a free will to act independently of his parents, he is held accountable for his actions without his parents at his side. "So then every one of us shall give account of himself to God" (Romans 14:12). There is no mention of father or mother giving account for the child or even being present with the child.

To summarize then, we have the analogy of faith, man's free will, individual accountability, divine comparisons (Isaiah 1:2 and the prodigal's father), generational choice (Ezekiel 18), and Adamic precedent (Adam sinned in the midst of perfection).

The conclusion is inescapable. Proverbs 22:6 cannot be interpreted as a promise only a general principle. Deterministic thinking around the teaching of parenting which is based on this verse needs to be revisited. In fact, there is no biblical basis for determinism in general. God's emphasis in Ezekiel 18 is consistent with the Word of God as a whole; every man is responsible for himself and no one else.

Confusing an Influence with a Cause

There are many human influences in a child's life which contribute to the fruit of his life but only one cause. Imagine a tree with much fruit in its limbs. There are many roots feeding into a common trunk. The fruit represents the actions of the child, the trunk represents the cause of those actions and the roots represent the influences. The influences are varied and many; the culture, the church, school, parents, peers, etc. The list is quite lengthy. And each of these roots have a potentially negative influence and/or a positive one.

For example, my father had some negative qualities but he also had some positive ones. One thing for which I am eternally grateful is that he taught me how to work and work hard. More than once, as a grade school kid, I put in long hours on the farm. On one occasion, my brother and I worked seventeen hours digging drainage ditches to rid the barnyard of flood water.

I regret to say that I chose to focus on Dad's negative qualities; the ones which I had used to justify running away from home. He wasn't very loving as a father. He came from the old school which never showed affection. He wasn't touchy-feely, huggy-wuggy, or even talky-walky, and so I concluded that he was incapable of love. Imagine my surprise years later as I watched my aged father care for my mother who was in the advanced stages of Alzheimer's. He brushed her hair, talked softly to her, fed her, and wiped her mouth. He then helped the nurse in getting her to bed. When he returned he sat down heavily with a sigh, and said,

"Jimmy, I have one prayer I pray constantly for your mom."
"What's that, Dad?" I asked. "To outlive her by one day."
For the first time, I saw the depth of my father's love. When she died, he was holding her hand, loving her to the end.

Why did I never see this? The answer is simple but embarrassing; I chose not to. I chose not to think on the things that are pure and lovely and of good report. Rather, I made a decision to dwell on the worst things in my Dad's character. I could have yielded myself a servant to righteousness, but I opted for sin unto death. (Romans 6:16).

My Dad had a positive side and a negative side. He influenced me in both ways, but I chose to think on the negative. This was the cause of my rebellion against him...my choice! Yes, he had an influence, but he did not cause me to sin. I did that without his help. Of course I wanted to blame him to justify myself and became quite expert at it. But until I separated his influence from the real cause of my sin, I never really found forgiveness and victory.

In his inimitable old school way, he eventually attempted reconciliation with me. I got a phone call that he was in the hospital with brain cancer and did not have long to live. I rushed to the Sweetwater, Tennessee hospital to see him. He was able to talk and seemed reflective as any man would who was facing his mortality. He was staring into space with tears in his eyes. "What's wrong, Dad?" I asked. He turned to look at me with the tears still precariously balanced on his eye lids. Looking deeply into my eyes, he said, "I have some regrets." The tears fell from their perch as the pride melted from his heart, and he gazed long and deep at me. He didn't have to say any more. I knew what he meant. He was apologizing for his harsh treatment of a sensitive little boy. "It's okay, Dad," I said. A moment of reconciliation I will always cherish.

Our last days together were good. Oh no, he was still not huggy-wuggy, but we had a respectful relationship until he died on a New Year's Eve. But I have often wondered, what if I had chosen differently?

Now I am a father. My son is in prison. I once asked him, "Son, did I ever let you down?" "Yeah, Dad," he replied. "When was that?" I asked. "You weren't there for me Dad. You always had time for church emergencies, and church people, but not for me." He was right. I had failed in my influence. I asked him to forgive me which he did readily. But to his credit, he has always insisted that what he has done is his fault and nobody else's. He recognizes the difference between an influence and a cause, even though he was deeply influenced by Fetal Alcohol Syndrome (FAS) passed on to him by his birthmother. (FAS is a condition which results in the child's diminished capacity in making decisions. See appendix)

Parents, we are responsible for our influence. We will answer to God for how we nurtured our children; how we taught them, prayed with them, whether we won them to Christ, took them to Sunday School, and whether we loved them. We must not shun our responsibilities in this regard; but at the same time, we dare not confuse our influence with the cause of our child's behavior. To fail in this is to fail our children.

If it's true that the teaching of rights brings rebellion and the teaching of responsibility brings revival, a compelling need of every child is to learn to take personal responsibility for his actions. To allow or even encourage blame-shifting, excusing of sin, justification for unrighteousness, etc., by conceding to the damnable doctrine of determinism is to aid and abet the enemy in the seduction of our children.

Chapter Eleven

How Do I Wash These Grape Stains Out?!

Helping Your Child Overcome Determinism
"...make you a new heart and a new spirit...
turn yourselves and live...: -Ezekiel 18:31-32

The cure for determinism is not simple, quick, or easy. Overcoming the temptation of blaming parents is an uphill battle. Like all spiritual growth, it is grounded in some raw-boned commitment to the truth and truthful thinking. This process begins with the mind which moves the heart, which moves the will. (See Appendix Six, "The Biblical Path of Lasting Change".) And the starting point for the mind must always be God Himself. This is the most important consideration before man for any change of thinking or living.

This is how God responds to the sour grapes advocates in Israel. His first statement after telling them they could no longer use their parents' sinfulness as an excuse for their own was to call attention to their view of Him. *"Behold, all souls are mine; as the soul of the father, so also the soul of the son is mine: the soul that sinneth, it shall die." (Ezekiel 18:4).*

In my many years of counseling, I have yet to confront a human problem which does not have its origin in a wrong image of God. By image of God, I mean what one believes about God, how they feel about God, how they relate to God, how they experience God, and how they view God in general. And I have never found a lasting cure for those problems which did not address this deeper one.

For example, anger is rooted in either distrust of God or disbelief in His sovereignty. If God is sovereign, and He is, then He is in control of all the circumstances of my life and all the people in my life (including my parents). If I get angry at the circumstances or people in my life, who am I really angry at? If I insist on being angry at my parents, do I really believe He's sovereign, or...

Do I believe that He's sovereign but don't really trust His sovereignty. It's really one or the other, isn't it? You can't believe Him and trust Him and get angry at the people or circumstances He has brought into your life.

Any attempt to deal with deep anger without addressing this root issue will not bring lasting change. Treatment of the fruit of life's tree will bring only temporary change.

The habits of life and belief are merely fruits on the upper branches of the tree; the image of God is the root. One can expend enormous time and effort picking the fruit, but it will grow back. So it does little lasting good to spend yourself in trying to stop acting in a wrong way.

This so discourages some that they revert to painting the fruit. Since they can't stop behaving wrongly, they hope at least to hide their sin by covering it with a shiny colorful coat of paint. But even the best paint can't stop the process of rot or the effort of worms to eat through it.

The answer is to get to the root, and the root is the image of God. This is where God begins in helping the Israelites. He addresses their view of His sovereignty; "You don't understand my sovereignty," He seems to say; "You don't realize how I take responsibility for you; for your heritage, your parentage, and your needs. "All souls are mine." Neither are you facing up to your responsibility to me as your God; the soul that sinneth, it shall die."

God has a master plan for the lives of every one of us. From your heritage to the number of hairs on your head, He is working His plan. You were born in the year of His design, you were born in the country of His choice, the state, the city, the hospital. *"Thou hast beset me behind and before, and laid thine hand upon me". (Psalm 139:5).* The color of your hair and skin were in His plan as were the shape of your fingers, your height, and the shape of your ears; *"I will praise thee; for I am fearfully and wonderfully made: marvellous are they works; and that my soul knoweth right well. My substance was not hid from thee, when I was made in secret, and curiously wrought in the lowest parts of the earth. Thine eyes did see my substance, yet being imperfect; and in thy book all my members were written, which in continuance were fashioned, when as yet there was none of them." (Psalm 139:14-16).* Everything in our lives, from the least significant to the most important is under God's Divine design.

And if it's true that *"children are an heritage of the LORD; and the fruit of the womb is his reward" (Psalm 127:3)*, that means that the children you have were God's choice for you. As Matthew Henry writes, *"...children are God's gift...If children are withheld, it is God that withholds them (Genesis 30:2); if they are given, it is God that gives them (Genesis 33:5); and they are to us what he makes them, comforts or crosses."*

If God has sovereignly appointed the children to the parents, it means He has also appointed the parents for the children. Good parents and bad parents alike are God's appointment for the children as much as good children and bad children alike ("comforts or crosses") are God's appointment for the parents. God has a plan, and whether He chooses to lead a child softly or expose him to harsh parenting, He is working out His plan.

I believe that I was born into the very home that God planned for me. I had the very parents He willed for me, and every circumstance I experienced under them was for a purpose. I could not know that purpose as an infant, and now as an adult, I know only what He has chosen to reveal to me. Everything else I accept by faith.

The same is true of you and your children. You must first believe this as a parent for yourself before you can fully believe it for them. Have you accepted God's sovereign design in placing you in the home of your parents? If not, how can you speak with conviction to your children about God placing them in your home? Have you fully embraced you children as God's choice for you? If not, how convincing can you be in teaching this to your children? Is your complete trust in God's wisdom and goodness in bringing parent and child together?

God takes full responsibility for this! He delights in your family because it's His creation. That is a hard truth for a child to understand when spiritual authority seems to be unfair, but it is true nonetheless.

I recall that as a child, after I had suffered unfairly at the hands of my father, I went out into the barnyard and looked up at a moonlit sky and growled in my anger; "God, if you're such a God of love, why are you letting this happen to an eight year old boy?!"

It was an accusation as much as it was a question, but God did have an answer. It took over twenty years for the answer to come but it did come and in an unexpected way. I was a pastor by then and found myself counseling a man who had been abused as a child. I found myself counseling him as I had been counseled, and encouraging him with the encouragement I had received. Then it hit me; this was God's purpose in my unfair treatment! This was all in God's design. He brought me through that so I could bring this man through this! *"Blessed be God...the Father of mercies, and the God of all comfort; Who comforteth us in all our tribulation, that we may be able to comfort them which are in any trouble, by the comfort wherewith we ourselves are*

131

comforted of God." (2 Corinthians 1:3-4). When I realized that this had increased my mercy and compassion, and had prepared me for a greater ministry than I could have imagined, anger at God was replaced by thanksgiving to God. I can now thank Him for the "unfair" spiritual authority He had put in my life.

The sooner a child can see with the eyes of faith and can envision God's higher purpose in allowing his pain, the sooner his trust in God will develop. Christ was facing the grossly unfair cruelty of the cross, but He was able to embrace it because He looked beyond it to the joy of being used to bring redemption to mankind. On that basis, we too are to embrace the sufferings of this present world; *"Looking unto Jesus the author and finisher of our faith; who for the joy that was set before him endured the cross, despising the shame, and is set down at the right hand of the throne of God. For consider him that endured such contradiction of sinners against himself, lest ye be wearied and faint in your minds." (Hebrews 12:2-3).* Jesus was treated unfairly by mankind, abused by His human authority, and even rejected by His own Heavenly Father when He "became sin for us," but through all the agony of the cross He knew that God had a grand design, that He was in control.

It is clear then that God takes full responsibility for us; for our creation, our placement in our homes, and for our every need. "All souls are mine". That is where our trust needs to be focused.

It is also clear that God desires each individual to take full responsibility for his sins and his alone; *"The soul that sinneth it shall die. The son shall not bear the iniquity of the father, neither shall the father bear the iniquity of the son: the righteousness of the righteous shall be upon him, and the wickedness of the wicked shall be upon him." (Ezekiel 18:20)*. Both the parent and the child must give account of himself to God. (Romans 14:12). Each will stand before God with a naked soul and no excuses. The child will not say, "But God, it's not my fault. It's the parent you gave me." It is to equip and prepare His children for their personal solo accountability to Him that God emphasizes the need of personal responsibility.

Each time a child is allowed or encouraged to blame someone else for his failures, he takes a step further away from personal responsibility, especially when that someone is a spiritual authority like his parents, especially when that spiritual authority is the father, because his relationship with his earthly father is a precursor of his relationship with his Heavenly Father. It is not by accident that Christ taught His disciples to pray thusly; *"Our Father which art in heaven..." (Matthew 6:9)*. To the Jews of a patriarchal society where fathers are admired and esteemed, it was a small step from obeying their earthly father and honoring their Heavenly Father. That is because their image of God had been shaped and molded by their earthly father. A lifetime of respect, reverence, and obedience to their earthly father prepared them for the transfer of obedience to the Heavenly Father. But a lifetime of disrespect, irreverence, and disobedience, even blaming of the earthly father, will retard an intimate relationship of trust with the Heavenly Father.

Conclusion

The sour grapes proverb of the Israelites is a myth, a lie concocted by the father of lies and embraced by misled generations. It has spawned more false guilt in parents and false innocence in children than any lie I know. It is not supported by the Word of God but by the wisdom of the world. It robs man of hope both for his children and as an adult child himself.

One can do no more than agree with God's assessment of the usage of it; *"As I live, saith the Lord God, ye shall not have occasion any more to use this proverb..." (Ezekiel 18:3).*

To adults I would ask; are you blaming your parents for your sins? Are you guilt-ridden over the sins of your children? Do you need to repent of a negative influence you have brought into your child's life? Do you need to seek their forgiveness for this? Are you in any way hindering God's conviction of your child by taking it upon yourself? Do you need to teach your child a biblical image of God? Are you teaching them to take responsibility for themselves? Do you need to trust God with your children and entrust Him with their outcome?

To the children I would ask; are you trusting God to work through your parents to accomplish His will in your life? Do you need to confess the sin of anger toward your parents and possibly toward God Himself? Are you willing to take personal responsibility for yourself?

I would recommend a thorough reading and study of this section on Sour Grapes along with a careful reading of Ezekiel chapter eighteen. One reading in one sitting will not benefit you like several exposures of the same truth.

Mike was being trained to be a football scout; to find and secure promising high school players for the state college. In preparation for this, he was taken to a high school football game by a veteran scout to learn the tricks of the trade. On the opening kick-off, a player went down and had to be carried off of a stretcher. Hoping to impress his instructor, Mike said, "Well, we don't want that guy, do we?!" On the next play another player went down and stayed down and Mike repeated his thought. This happened several more times. After Mike said "we don't want that guy, do we?!" for the umpteenth time, his instructor said, "No! I want the guy knocking everybody down!"

The Bible exhorts us; *"Be not overcome of evil, but overcome evil with good" (Romans 12:21).* Every parent has a choice. Congratulate yourself for merely getting back up, or becoming the victor. The devil wants you to adopt a passive, re-active mindset. God wants you to take an active, aggressive role in overcoming evil in your family and leading

your children spiritually. You are on the winning side!
Never forget that!

Appendix Number One

What You Should Know About Attention Deficit Disorder (ADD)
by Edward T. Welch, Ph.D.

Concerned and puzzled parents have made ADD the best known psychiatric diagnosis ever. Books on the topic in public libraries seldom return to the shelves – waiting lists keep them almost perpetually checked out.[1] In an effort to better understand and help their children, parents have turned to seminars, news reports, and TV shows for information. Computer networks even have bulletin boards devoted to the topic. To add to this interest, many adults are finding that ADD applies to them, too. Adults who are intellectually capable but "never measured up to their potential" have found in ADD a category that makes all the seemingly disparate pieces of their lives finally fit together. Rarely does any literature leave so many readers thinking, "So that's the problem?"

As with everything we read and hear, Christians should assimilate this information with biblical discernment.

The material on ADD is often interesting and helpful, but it is not Scripture. Therefore, it can be prone to unbiblical assumptions and errors. For example, some books on ADD abolish the words "bad" or "sinful." Other books are less interested in an objective interpretation of the research than they are in doing everything possible to bolster a child's self-esteem. Other books use a biological approach, claiming that brain functioning explains every behavior. What follows is an overview and some biblical guidelines with which to understand ADD.

Definitions of ADD

The technical definition of ADD has evolved over the last few decades. Its present form highlights two symptoms: inattention and hyperactivity-impulsivity.[2] To receive the label you must have one, the other, or both, as seen in the following definition:

A. Either (1) or (2):

(1) Six (or more) of the following symptoms of inattention have persisted for at least six months to a degree that is maladaptive and inconsistent with developmental level:

Inattention

Often makes careless mistakes in school work, work, or other activities.

Often has difficulty sustaining attention in tasks or play

activities.

Often does not seem to listen when spoken to directly.

Often does not follow-through on instructions and fails to finish schoolwork, chores, or duties in the work place (not due to oppositional behavior or failure to understand instructions).

Often has difficulty organizing tasks and activities.

Often avoids, dislikes, or is reluctant to engage in tasks that require sustained mental effort (such as schoolwork or homework).

Often loses things necessary for tasks or activities (e.g. toys, school assignments, pencils, or tools).

Is often easily distracted by extraneous stimuli.

Is often forgetful in daily activities.

(2) Six (or more) of the following symptoms of hyperactivity-impulsivity have persisted for at least six months to a degree that is maladaptive and inconsistent with development level:

Hyperactivity

Often fidgets with hands or feet or squirms in seat.

Often leaves seat in classroom or in other situations in which remaining seated is expected.

Often runs about or climbs excessively in situations in which it is inappropriate (in adolescents or adults, may be limited to subjective feelings of restlessness).

Often has difficulty playing or engaging in leisure activities quietly.

Is often "on the go" or often acts as if "driven by a motor."

Often talks excessively.

Impulsivity

Often blurts out answers before questions have been completed.

Often has difficulty awaiting turn.

Often interrupts or intrudes on others (e.g., butts into conversations or games).

B. Some hyperactive-impulsive or inattentive symptoms that caused impairment were present before age 7 years.

C. Some impairment from the symptoms is present in two or more settings (e.g., at school [or work] and at home).

D. There must be clear evidence of clinically significant impairment in social, academic, or occupational functioning.

Such children (and adults) seem to have mouths (and arms, hands, and legs!) that run ahead of their thinking. Or, their thinking is distracted and darts from one place to another. Their bodies are just trying to keep up. Caring for young boys who fit these descriptions make you feel as if you are spinning a dozen plates in the air. Parents often manage the problem by withdrawing their children from situations where they will embarrass them or be too rough with other children. In the case of younger girls, their symptoms tend to be less noticeable because, while they may be highly distractible, they are less likely to be hyperactive. As a result, they stare out the classroom windows, don't' disturb their classmates, and go unnoticed for years.

Older children can be maddening in that they can be fixated on the TV for hours, but they can concentrate on their homework for ten seconds or less. (TV and Nintendo give them a fast pace and excitement; homework does not).

In other words, their attention is inconsistent rather than universally poor. For these children boredom is death. They might provoke Mom or engage in some physically dangerous activity just to make life more interesting.

The adults have lives that are often characterized by chronic difficulties meeting deadlines, frequent job changes (they are either bored or fired), impulsive decisions, inaccurate insights into personal strengths and weaknesses, and inaccurate insights into the ways that others respond to them.

With these descriptions it is easy to understand why there is so much interest in ADD. Parents, as well as adults, who loosely fit the profile, are looking for anything that will help.

Cautions With ADD

Before outlining a biblical plan of action, I would offer two cautions to keep in mind with ADD. First, ADD is not a precisely circumscribed set of symptoms. The ever-present "often" in the diagnostic criteria betrays the loose boundaries of ADD, and it explains why Americans use the diagnosis so frequently.[3] Almost anyone can squeeze into these parameters – at least on certain days. Given such imprecision it would be more accurate to see ADD behaviors on a continuum rather than on an all-or-nothing grid ("yes, he has ADD," or "no, he does not have it"). Everyone can find themselves somewhere on the continuum, but there is no question that some people are more consistently at the extremes.

Second, ADD is a description of behavior, not an explanation. It tries to describe symptoms rather than explain the causes of those symptoms. It tries to answer the question, "What is this child doing?" but not, "Why is this child doing it?" These two questions are very different. For example, if you were new to the automotive world and asked about a car you just saw speeding by, a descriptive or "what" answer would be, "That was a dark green Ford Taurus Station Wagon with a 2.0 liter engine." An explanatory or "why" answer, however, would review the basics of combustion engines and the mechanics of automatic transmissions.

ADD descriptions begin to answer what the child is doing, not why. These what descriptions can certainly be helpful. For example, if you want to understand what specific behaviors contribute to your child's poor school performance, then the symptom list associated with the term ADD might reveal behaviors that you had not previously considered. Yet this descriptive category is limited in its usefulness. It would not be helpful if someone asked, "Why is your son always squirming in his chair?" If you responded, "Because he has ADD," that is really no different than saying, "He squirms in his chair because he fidgets." You are merely describing his behaviors with different vocabulary.

The reason it is important to distinguish between description and explanation is that the ADD literature typically does not distinguish between them. Most discussions about ADD assume that the list of descriptions is equivalent to establishing a medical diagnosis. The popular assumption is that there is an underlying biological cause for the behaviors, but the assumption is unfounded. Although there are dozens of biological theories to explain ADD, there are presently no physical markers for it; there are no medical tests that detect its presence. Food additives, birth and delivery problems, inner ear problems, and brain differences are only a few of the theories that are intriguing but unsupported by evidence. Each may have some merit in specific cases, but there is no one biological theory that can consistently explain the symptoms. At this point we can't say that anyone has ADD in the way that someone has a virus.

Why then are the biological explanations so intertwined with the descriptions? First, for some people, biological explanations are assumed to be the only explanation available for behavior. They know of no other causes. Second, some investigators are concerned that any moral judgments might damage a child. They have seen children hurt by the capricious (and unbiblical) punishment of "bad" children. In order to raise "self-esteem," these researchers want to avoid any suggestion that children are responsible for ADD behaviors.

Since there is such a close connection between the label ADD and the biological hypotheses, we should be alert to how we use the phrase.

Your Child and Ritalin

Andy's mom and dad didn't want to give him Ritalin. They believed that their child was normal and that with proper discipline and consistent love he would outgrow his problems adjusting to school. But the school psychologist said that Andy suffered from attention deficit-hyperactivity disorder (ADHD). He warned that Andy would need special classes if he didn't go to a physician to get Ritalin.

After a ten-minute discussion with Andy's mom, the family pediatrician prescribed two doses of Ritalin each day, one before school and one at lunch break to be given by the school nurse. Within a week, Mom noticed that Andy was more "hyperactive" than ever in the evening. Because no one had warned her that Andy's brain might "bounce back" from the medication, resulting in increased hyperactivity later in the day, she thought that her son's condition must be getting worse.

The pediatrician may not have known that Ritalin and other stimulants commonly make children more agitated and excited as they wear off in the evening. In response to a brief phone call from Andy's mother, he added a later afternoon dose of Ritalin for a total of three per day.

The third dose of Ritalin seemed to work. According to the afternoon baby sitter, when Andy got home from school he took his Ritalin right away and then went upstairs to watch TV or to do his homework. But within a week, the parents discovered that Andy was staying up all night. Now the doctor added Dalmane as a sleeping pill.

One morning, Andy's mom and dad looked with dismay at their son at the breakfast table. Their hearts sank at the sight of the listless, sad-faced little fellow. They decided to stop all his medications but didn't know how to go about it. After a consultation with a second pediatrician who wanted to put Andy on another stimulant, Adderall, Andy's mom and dad decided to seek help from a doctor who was critical of the practice of giving stimulants to children and who supported the parents' efforts to wean Andy from prescription medications.

The new pediatrician explained the various Ritalin withdrawal effects to both Andy and his parents, encouraged them to stay in close touch, and tapered the boy from Ritalin. As the dose was reduced, Andy no longer needed the Dalmane to sleep. Within a couple of weeks, Andy's mom and dad felt that their child had been restored to them.

Instead of sending Andy back to the public school, his parents enrolled him in a private school that prided itself in individualizing its programs to the needs of its students. To their joy, the child who "needed Ritalin" in the public school did fine in the private school from the very first day of class. In retrospect, they were appalled at how close they had come to subjecting their child to years of drugging in order to make him conform to the local school system.

> - Your Drug May Be Your Problem,
> Perseus Press, Peter Breggin, M.D.

Peter R. Breggin, M.D., has become an internationally-known psychiatrist and author of a dozen books, including Talking Back to Prozac, Toxic Psychiatry, and Talking Back to Ritalin. The International Director of the Center for the Study of Psychiatry and Psychology, which he founded in the early 1970s, Dr. Breggin lives in Bethesda, Maryland.

Website: www.breggin.com,

(301) 652-5954, breggin@tmn.com

How To Help

If someone suggests that your child (or you) displays behaviors consistent with ADD, don't panic. Translate ADD as, "It is time to develop a deeper understanding of this person."

There are at least two areas that must be investigated: the spiritual and the physical. Both must be taken seriously. If you ignore the spiritual, there will never be a place for repentance and faith in your child's life. Sinful behavior will be excused. The power of the gospel will be ignored. If you ignore physical or brain-based strengths and weaknesses, you will never find the creative methods you need to help your child learn. The child will soon be confused and hopeless.

The spiritual is the realm of the heart or spirit. It is the very essence of our being, deeper even than what we consider our personality. The heart emphasizes that we live before God and either worship God in faith and obedience or follow our own desires. When we worship or obey God, our hearts express themselves in love, joy, peace, patience, kindness, gentleness, and self-control. (Galatians 6:19-23) When we are committed to or worship our own desires, the acts of the sinful nature are apparent. These include arguments, complaining, jealousy, fits of rage, sexual immorality, and disobedience to parents.

With my children labeled ADD, the arena of the heart is ignored. Yet isn't it possible that some of what we call ADD is sinful self-indulgence and laziness? Is it possible that a prominent cause of the behaviors is a heart that demands its own way? It certainly is possible. The truth is that ADD sits at a theological intersection where physical and spiritual meet. The root cause may be physical or spiritual; it is typically both.

Does it sound harsh to suggest that sin may be a cause

of what is popularly called ADD? Might such an explanation damage children as some secular investigators suggest? I think not. If sin is called sin, it can give hope for change. Furthermore, most children have a conscience that is alert to right and wrong. To say that something is wrong is to tell them something they already suspect. What can be hurtful and confusing is when something is called sinful or wrong, but it should more accurately be called a limitation or weakness.

One way to avoid confusing sin and personal limitation or weakness is to ask the question, "Am I certain that this behavior transgresses God's law?" If so, then the behavior is rooted in a spiritual problem. Say, for example, your child is playing with his toy. This is clearly a spiritual problem. Your child might also struggle with inattention and hyperactivity-impulsivity, but these cannot be excuses for such behavior. Physical problems do not force a child to sin.

Physical problems, however, certainly influence behavior. Furthermore, they can be mistaken for spiritual problems. Therefore, while trying to understand the orientation of the child's heart (either toward God or self) you will also be trying to understand the child's unique physical (brain-based) strengths and weaknesses.

The physical is the material person – muscles, bone, brain, and genes. In a sense our physical being is the equipment for our heart. It gives our heart a means of expression in a physical world. This physical endowment is different from the heart in that while the heart is obedient or sinful, the body is strong or weak.

In a child labeled ADD, these physical strengths (talents, abilities) might include a high energy level, unusual creativity, a willingness to take risks, and an outgoing personality.

Physical weaknesses, sometimes apparent in ADD-labeled children, include a poor memory for the spoken or written word, difficulty sequencing behavior or devising steps to complete a task, difficulty establishing priorities, difficulty with sustained attention when tasks are not intrinsically interesting, difficulty screening out irrelevant stimuli, and difficulty changing from one way of thinking to another.

An example of this last weakness is the child who is loud and active at home and carries that same behavior into the classroom. Such children had difficulties when the rules change. They might be spiritually teachable but mentally inflexible.

Although these two categories of physical and spiritual are distinct, discerning the way each of them contributes to troublesome behavior can be challenging. Let's say, for example, that you told your child to clean his room. When you return twenty minutes later, he is still playing with toys amid the chaos. Is this a spiritual problem? On the surface it would certainly seem so. The child has violated the command to obey his parents. Yet there might be other explanations. Perhaps the child does not know how to "clean his room" – the idea might be too general and abstract. Perhaps his rooms look perfectly clean to him, or perhaps he started to clean the room and then got distracted by a favorite toy. In other words, what you may be seeing is a weakness in the child's ability to follow through with the directions rather than intentional disobedience.

There is a difference between telling a child to "clean your room" and "don't hit your brother." The child has a conscience and intuitively knows that he should not hit others in anger. Such an act would be wrong even if a parent did not say "don't hit." But the child does not have a conscience that says it is morally wrong to leave a messy room. The messy room is technically a violation of the command to obey parents, but in some cases disobedience is not the relevant biblical category. An understanding of the child's heart might indicate that the problems are physical limitations and ignorance, not spiritual rebellion. In other words there are never excuses for sinful anger and unloving behavior, but there are times when there are excuses for not cleaning your room.

What if a child is disruptive at a dinner table? It may be that the child is naturally more active but is also unwilling to listen to parental instruction. In such cases the parent must know how to address both a sinful heart and an energetic constitution. All of a sudden parenting is becoming complicated!

But a biblical perspective simplifies. Biblical parenting is time-consuming, and it relies on counsel from others, but it is not necessarily complicated. With the distinction between physical and spiritual problems in mind, take steps to grow in nurturing your child in the Lord. No matter what your child's strengths and weaknesses, she has the same spiritual problem as everyone else: her heart is in a war between selfishness and obedience to Christ. How does she fight? With (1) the knowledge of Christ and (2) obedience to Christ. The knowledge of Christ consists of learning about the great justice and love of God displayed in Jesus' death and resurrection. Obedience to Christ is our response to this good news. It consists of practicing the command to love your neighbor as yourself, a command that is fleshed out by the Ten Commandments and other clear principles in Scriptures.

For children who tend to be more impulsive in their speech or actions, there are some biblical principles that might deserve special emphasis. The parental task is to develop priorities among the various biblical principles and stay focused on those that are most important for the child's spiritual needs. It is wiser to take one principle and work with it intensively for a few months than it is to work with ten principles superficially, leaving them undeveloped, unclear, and not regularly prayed for.

James 1:19 is a passage of Scripture that is at the top of many parents' lists. It is uniquely suited to those who tend to be more distractible and impulsive: "Wherefore my beloved brethren, let every man be swift to hear, slow to speak, slow to wrath." This triad may take years to master; but if God requires such behaviors, He will give grace to accomplish them.

As these children move into teen and adult years, other principles might become more important. Since adolescents have minds that tend to fly from one thing to another or prefer the spontaneous to the planned and orderly, it might be especially important for these teens to learn the biblical principle of perseverance. Other teens and adults might be horrible at prioritizing work or consistently overestimate their ability to do a particular task. Such people must learn the biblical principle of being teachable and seeking the counsel of others: "Without counsel purposes are disappointed: but in the multitude of counselors they are established." (Proverbs 15:22)

As you gain proficiency in spiritual nurture and discipleship, turn your attention to the person's unique strengths and weaknesses. Start by getting as much information on your child as possible. Don't be embarrassed; talk with school teachers, Sunday School teachers, babysitters, and friends. Ask the school for educational testing. The more you understand the particular strengths and weaknesses of the person, the better you can creatively teach and apply relevant biblical principles. For example, if your child does better with pictures and concrete, visual explanations than he does with oral instructions, you might role-play how to be kind to a younger sibling rather than tell him that he should "be kind." "Hear it, see it, do it" is the parent's or educator's rule of thumb.

Many of the practical suggestions for dealing with those who are distractible or tend to bounce from one activity to another can be summarized with the word structure.

Structure refers to boundaries, guidelines, reminders and limits. It is a fence that can help contain and direct. Since some children have a style of thinking that is chaotic, disorganized and unreliable, structure compensates by providing external controls. Without structure, the constant change and ambiguous expectations aggravate every small difficulty.

Structure means having predictable, clear, simple and written household rules. These rules should be rehearsed weekly with the child and consistently enforced. Avoid lengthy, abstract explanations. If you need time to develop a particular teaching or explain a form of discipline, try to dialogue with the child as a way to put boundaries on his attention. Ask questions. Have him read Scripture out loud. Ask him to explain where he disobeyed. When giving instructions, make sure the child is listening; have her look at you and ask her to repeat the instructions. You might even review her plan for carrying out the instructions.

Structure means that instead of constantly reacting to problems, which can increase the sense of chaos, you preempt them. Although the child may have difficulties anticipating problems ahead, you should be alert to the places where he habitually stumbles. You know from experience where there will be difficulties. If the difficult situation cannot or should not be avoided, prepare the child to face it with prayer and practice. Then, after the difficult time is over (e.g., homework, chores), give the child feedback so he can see his progress.

For the adult who tends to have difficulty paying attention or making plans, structure means establishing routines such as doing three difficult but necessary tasks before more enjoyable jobs. It means to set reasonable deadlines (under the guidance of others) and meet them. Well-prioritized "to do" lists are a must.

Medical Treatments

If you have diligently pursued these suggestions but are still troubled by the severity of a child's hyperactivity or distractibility, especially if those behaviors are dramatically affecting school performance, then you might consult with a knowledgeable physician. There are some medical problems that can provoke ADD symptoms. For example, thyroid problems can affect energy level, and hearing or visual impairments can make paying attention difficult. A good physical exam can rule these out.

The vast majority of ADD-labeled children will have normal physical exams, but many physicians suggest a medical treatment anyway. The treatment is typically stimulant drugs such as Ritalin or antidepressants such as Norpramin (Desipramine) or Prozac.

That a stimulant drug would help some children focus seems paradoxical. You would expect that children would be even more physically and mentally excitable when taking it. However, at the commonly prescribed doses, everyone tends to have better performance on certain simple mental tasks, and children in particular seem to be less fidgety.

154

How does Ritalin do this? We know that Ritalin affects a number of areas in the brain, but its mode of action is uncertain. One thing, however, is clear. Ritalin does not treat any known chemical deficiency in a child's brain. No one needs Ritalin. The most generous analogy would be to say that Ritalin-type drugs act like aspirin; they suppress symptoms in some people, but they are not a cure.

Most experts agree that Ritalin-type drugs are over-prescribed. They argue that ADD itself is over-diagnosed, that our culture is quick to treat any behavior with drugs and that physicians are quick to dispense such a relatively safe drug to children whose parents are looking for a quick solution. This does not mean that we must avoid the drug. It does mean, however, that, as the American Pediatric Association suggests, we consider it after examining other factors in the child's life. Should Christian parents consider this medication for their children? If you consult with a cross-section of the Christian population, you will hear "definitely yes," "definitely no, and under no circumstances," and everything in between. Such differences of opinion among committed, thinking Christians suggest, at least, that Scripture does not clearly say "no." The question is more "Is it wise?" than "Is it wrong?"

In order to make a wise choice, there is information to consider. Ritalin is one of the safe prescription drugs. It was first used with hyperactive children in the 1930s, so it has a long history; it is presently prescribed to over two million people, so we are familiar with its side effects.

The most common side effects of Ritalin are the suppression of appetite and loss of sleep. Since these side effects are dose-related, they can sometimes be avoided by lowering the dose. Another troubling though rare side effect are involuntary muscle twitches. These, too, might disappear with a lower dose. If not, they will disappear when the medication is discontinued.

At its best Ritalin can help an individual focus better, sustain efforts over a longer period of time, moderate mood swings, and reduce distractibility. At its worst it has side effects without beneficial effects.

It was once assumed that Ritalin improved school performance, yet the evidence does not support this assumption. Although Ritalin is praised by many elementary school teachers, and some children demonstrate significant behavioral changes, there is very little evidence that Ritalin significantly improves school performance. After two years of taking Ritalin, most children who receive the drug perform at about the same level as the ADD-labeled counterparts who do not receive it.

It is imperative to stress that drugs cannot change a child's heart. If a child seems more obedient when taking Ritalin, it is because an influence on the child's life has changed. That is, in the same way that parents and peers can influence our hearts, so our bodies can influence us. Our bodies bring pleasure and pain, intellectual clarity and confusion. Such physical changes can act like a temptation to which some children given in and respond sinfully. When the temptation is removed, these children might seem less prone to certain kinds of sins.

If you do choose to try Ritalin-type drugs, the most important principle to maintain is that your quest for medical treatment must not outdistance your diligence in spiritual nurture. No matter how profound the physical weaknesses may be, they cannot keep your child from growing in the knowledge of Christ and obedience. That fact should offer hope and encouragement in the discipling of your child as well as limit your expectations about what medications will do for him.

Some parents seek alternative medical treatments such as diet or megavitamins. Wisdom is again the rule. If you pursue these treatments, don't let them substitute for spiritual nurture, and be careful how much time and money you invest. They are helpful only in very select cases.

Parenting those with ADD symptoms is ultimately like parenting any child – you accommodate your biblical instruction to the child's abilities. With children who are like us, such parenting is relatively straightforward because we instinctively understand their strengths and weaknesses. Children whose strengths and weaknesses are out of the mainstream, however, take more careful observation and creative teaching. With these children remember that they too have God-given strengths, and whatever weaknesses they have will not slow their growth in those things that are most important.

A Doctor Looks At Ritalin

The Child's Feelings are Disregarded

The actual impact of stimulants on the brain and mind of children are poorly understood, and despite administering the drug to millions of youngsters in the past several years, psychiatry shows little interest in the question. In none of the many standard and even specialized textbooks I consulted could I find any interest in how children feel when taking stimulants. The subjective experience of the child is ignored. It is as if we are putting coins (instead of pills) into one end of a black box (instead of a child) and getting an output at the other end. What happens inside the box is of no concern; all we care about is the behavioral end product. This disregard for the person's subjective response is due in part to the stigmatitization of the patients: not only are they "mental patients," they are children. That they are involuntary patients makes it all the easier, and in some ways necessary, to ignore their feelings.

The study "Why Johnny Can't Sit Still" Kids' Ideas on Why They Take Stimulants," was conducted by [two] physicians . . . [one of which] is an experienced researcher from the Division of Neuropsychiatry at Walter Reed. . . . the authors systematically evaluated twenty children given Ritalin by their primary care physicians.

Many of the children thought they were taking the pill to "control them" because they were "bad." They often attributed their conduct to outside forces, such as eating sugar or not taking their pill, rather than to themselves. The researchers conclude that taking the drugs produced (1) "defective superego formation" manifested by "disowning responsibility for their provocation behavior;" (2) "impaired self-esteem development;" (3) "lack of resolution of critical family events which preceded the emergence of the child's hyperactive behavior;" and (4) displacement of "family difficulties onto the child."

Chemical Imbalance?

The idea that Ritalin and other stimulants correct biochemical imbalances in the brain of hyperactive children, although promoted by Wender and others, is false on two counts. First, there is no known biochemical imbalance in these children, and second, it generally is accepted that Ritalin has the same effect on all individuals, regardless of their psychiatric diagnosis or behavior.

Side Effects

Frequently listed side effects are sadness or depression, social withdrawal, flattened emotions, and loss of energy. Consistent with the brain-disabling principle of biopsychiatric treatment . . . I believe that these subduing effects are not side effects the primary "therapeutic effect," rendering the child less troublesome and easier to manage. [The brain-disabling principle applies to all of the most potent psychiatric treatments – neuroleptics, antidepressants, lithium, electroshock, and psychosurgery. The principle states that all of the major psychiatric treatments exert their primary or intended effect by disabling normal brain function.)

Cocaine in Disguise?

The Drug Enforcement Administration (DEA) puts Ritalin . . . in Class II, along with morphine, barbiturates, and other prescription drugs that have a high potential for addiction or abuse. Goodman and Gilman's The Pharmacological Basis of Therapeutics (1985) points out that Ritalin is "structurally related to amphetamine" and says simply, "Its pharmacological properties are essentially the same as those of the amphetamines" (p. 586). It considers Ritalin among the highly addictive drugs.

Brain Damage From Ritalin?

There is reason to be concerned about brain tissue shrinkage as a result of long-term Ritalin therapy . . . [An article] in Psychiatric Research, found [this] brain pathology in more than half of twenty-four young adults. Since all of the patients had been treated with psychostimulants, "cortical atrophy may be a long-term adverse effect of this treatment." (p. 245) One study is suggestive rather than conclusive, but there remains a cause for concern. It bears repeating that the use of any potent psychoactive drug is not good for the brain.

Does Ritalin Help?

While psychostimulants can blunt a child sufficiently to make him more amenable to control in a classroom or at home, at least for a few weeks, there is little or no evidence of any beneficial long-term effect on academic or psychosocial life.

In evaluating the impact of Ritalin, the importance of the placebo effect must be taken into account. As the American Psychiatric Press Textbook of Psychiatry points out, while as many as 75 percent of children are rated improved during the initial treatment (and subduing) phase with Ritalin, 40 percent of placebo or nondrug controls are rated similarly. This suggests that placebo may account for more than 50 percent of the supposed Ritalin effect.

- Toxic Psychiatry, St. Martin's Press by Peter Breggin, M.D.
- Chapter 13

Appendix Number Two

Scriptural Evaluation
of Salvation Invitations

"Will you give your heart to Christ?" This invitation is misleading. The Scriptures never tell us to give our heart to Christ. Such an invitation implies some effort on our part. We are not saved by giving God anything, but rather by receiving His gift of eternal life. (Ephesians 2:8 -9). Even so, this invitation contains very confusing terminology that does not clearly present the truth of the gospel.

"Will you surrender your life to Christ?" Surrender implies "giving everything" to the Lord, while salvation is accepting the work of Christ on our behalf as a free gift. This invitation is the reverse of scriptural teaching. We are saved by receiving rather than by giving (John 1:12). The appeal of surrender is fitting only for a believer to yield his life to obedient service to the Lord. Such an appeal cannot be used for salvation. The expression "yield" in Romans 6 and "present" in Romans 12, both of which apply to believers, are calls to obedience and the need for dedicating one's life to God's will. Do not confuse these expressions and concepts with accepting and believing for salvation.

"Will you come to Christ tonight and promise to serve Him from now on?" The promise to serve Christ has meaning only for the believer. No invitation for service could be given to the unsaved because he has no spiritual life (Ephesians 2:1). Also, the idea of "coming to Christ" may give the thought of trying to make oneself acceptable to Christ. If "coming" means deciding to accept Christ and His finished work on the cross, however, such an invitation may be acceptable. This invitation contains vague terminology, though, and will very likely be misunderstood by the unsaved person. The promise to serve Him is unacceptable for salvation because it gives the idea of works (Ephesians 2:8-9). Serving the Lord is a result of being saved. Service has nothing to do with getting saved.

"Right now ask Jesus to come into your heart." We are not saved by Jesus coming into our hearts but rather by trusting in His death for us (Ephesians 1:7). When we believe, He does indwell us. Our body then becomes the temple of the Holy Spirit. However that is a result of salvation. It is not the method whereby we are saved. Children find it confusing because they wonder if Jesus can physically come into their hearts. The simplicity of believing and trusting is misunderstood. Revelation 3:20 is often the basis of this invitation. Yet, this passage does not deal with salvation. It does not focus the attention on Christ dying in my place and my acceptance of His work for me.

"Will you make your commitment for Christ tonight?"
This is one of the most misleading, vague invitations imaginable. A "commitment to Christ" could mean any number of things, such as serving, breaking wicked habits, obeying, making greater effort to do right, changing friends, or changing my life-style. Committing or promising something to God is certainly a "work" on my part. The unsaved person who is dead in trespasses and sin is unable to make any kind of commitment whatsoever. We are not saved by our promises to God, but by believing Christ's work is for us. (John 3:18). The unsaved person needs a new life in Christ. Only when he places his faith in the finished work of Christ will he receive that life in Christ (1 John 5:12).

-Adopted from an Awana Fact Sheet

Appendix Number Three

Ten Reasons Adopted Children Have More Conflicts

Causes of Conflicts	Steps of Action
1. They are affected by the sins of their natural parents, and these sins are usually very severe (Romans 5:12, Exodus 20:5.)	1. Acknowledge to God the sins of the natural parents, and ask Him to remove their destructive influences (Leviticus 26:40-42, Nehemiah 1:6, 9:2, Psalm 106:6, Jeremiah 14:20, Daniel 9:4-20.)
2. Adoptive parents are usually unprepared to counteract inborn weaknesses and tendencies in adopted children.	2. Learn the physical and spiritual weakness of the natural parents, and establish corresponding disciplines (Exodus 20:6, Deuteronomy 12:28.) Find out all you can about parents' sins.
3. They have greater conflicts with rejection (Jephthah – Judges 11:1-40.)	3. Explain and illustrate that God has a special purpose for their lives (Moses, Joseph, Samuel, Esther – Romans 8:28-29.)
4. They usually have conflicts with natural-born brothers or sisters because parents try to treat them all alike (II Thessalonians 2:11.)	4. Explain the key to their success – having a servant's spirit. Motivate them to see the family as God's special "classroom" (Mark 10:43-45, Proverbs 17:2.)

Causes of Conflicts	Steps of Action
5. They tend to have a bitter spirit because of the circumstances of their births (Hebrews 12:15.)	5. Lead them to thank God for His purposes in removing their natural parents, and focus on benefits. Understand salvation (Ephesians 1:5) God's special care (Psalm 27:10, 68:5) Special life purpose (Psalm 139) Identify with Christ's rejection by others (John 8:41)
6. They are often adopted in order to meet the emotional needs of the adoptive parents rather than their needs (as a result, the child knows or senses he can demand much because of the parents' need of his presence.)	6. Make a total dedication of each child to the Lord. Treat children as loans from God (Psalm 127:3, Genesis 22, I Samuel 1.)
7. They often free adoptive mothers emotionally to have their own children, who are then favored over them (I Samuel 1:10, II Samuel 6:16-23.)	7. Determine if your desire for a child is God's preparation for a "special child." Mentally and emotionally consecrate yourselves and any children to God (Isaac, Jacob, Joseph, Samuel, Samson, and John the Baptist were all born to "barren" mothers.)
8. They often discover that some family members had opposed their adoption. These members look for faults to prove that they were right.	8. Discuss adoption with the entire family. Ask God for clear signs of His leading. Wait for family to be in full agreement on adoption.

Causes of Conflicts	Steps of Action
9. They often have conflicting loyalties when they desire to find their natural parents, and they know that this will hurt their adoptive parents.	9. Cooperate with an adopted child's need to learn about his or her natural parents. Point out the parents' positive qualities as well as spiritual needs. Teach the child to love and pray for their natural parents.
10. They tend to lack self-worth if they were the result of immorality.	10. Teach adopted children to follow Christ's example by identifying with their heavenly Father more than with their earthly father.

Appendix Number Four

Words that Hurt or Heal an Adopted Child

By Sherrie Eldridge & Jody Moreen

Words that Hurt	How Adoptee May Translate	What God Says	Words that Heal
"Given up for adoption."	I was alone. I didn't belong to anybody.	*Psalm 71:6b* "*...thou art he that took me out of my mother's bowels: ...*" *Psalm 68:5* "*A father of the fatherless ...*" *Psalm 27:10* "*When my father and my mother forsake me, then the LORD will take me up.*	Make an adoption plan. It must be sad to think about the time when your birthmother said good-bye. There was Someone else there with you all the time, even though you couldn't see Him. It was Jesus. He was with you then and is with us now. He promises never to leave you.
"This is my adopted daughter." (introduction)	I am different.	*Matthew 3:17* "*And lo a voice from heaven, saying, This is my beloved Son, in whom I am well pleased*	This is my daughter.
"Illegitimate"	I have no right to be alive.	*Jeremiah 1:5* "*Before I formed thee in the belly I knew thee; and before thou camest forth out of the womb I sanctified thee, and I ordained thee a prophet unto the nations.*"	God is the Creator of all life. You are here because He created you and has a special plan for your life.
"We couldn't have our own kids, so we adopted you."	I'm second choice and second best. If I'm not their own, where do I belong? Am I an alien?	*Psalm 139:16:b* "*And in thy book all my members were written, which in continuance were fashioned, when as yet there was none of them.*"	God formed our family through adoption. You are His jewel and ours

Words that Hurt	How Adoptee May Translate	What God Says	Words that Heal
"Be thankful you were a chosen child."	I must always act happy that I was adopted. If I don't, I will seem ungrateful or disloyal.	*Romans 11:24* "...*thou wert cut out of the olive three which is wild by nature, and wert grafted contrary to nature into a good olive tree...*"	Adoption is a mysters—it is both wonderful and painful. I want to hear about all your feelings— sad, mad, glad, and scared.
"Your birthmother gave you up because she loved you."	I am afraid you will abandon me too because you say you love me. How can that be? You don't give up someone if you love them.	*Isaiah 49:15-16* "*Can a woman forget her sucking child, that she should not have compassion on the son of her womb? Yea, they may forget, yet will I not forget thee. Behold, I have graven thee upon the palms of my hands...*"	We don't know why your birthmother left. Some things in life are hard to understand. It must hurt. God will never leave you, nor will we (adoptive parents)
"Why did your birthmother leave?"	I must have been a bad baby. I must be really good so I don't get left behind again.	*Psalm 127:3* "*Lo, children are an heritage of the Lord, and the fruit of the womb is his reward.*"	We don't know the reasons why she left, but we believe it must have been very sad for her to part with a precious baby like you. We are glad she gave you the gift of life and then gave you to us 0 you are our jewel from God. Why don't we pray and ask God to take care of her?
"Unplanned pregnancy"	I am a mistake	*Isaiah 55:8* "*For my thoughts are not your thoughts, neither are your ways my ways, saith the Lord.*"	Your life story began long ago, in eternity past, in the heart of God. He planned your life even if your birthparents didn't.

Words that Hurt	How Adoptee May Translate	What God Says	Words that Heal
(A quivering lip)	Asking about my birth and birthparents upsets Mommy. I'd better keep quiet.	*John 8:32* "And ye shall know the truth and the truth shall make you free."	(Warm smile.) I will tell you as much as I know. (age appropriate)
"When you're older, we'll talk about your birth and birth family."	I shouldn't ask about this again. It must be ugly and bad. What is so difficult that it must be withheld from me?	*Exodus 4:14* "Is not Aaron the Levite your brother?"	It's very normal for an adoptee to wonder about his/her birth family. Moses was an adoptee, and God stirred up questions in his heart about his birth brother, Aaron. Tell me, what do you think your birth family is like?
"You look just like us," or "you are just like us." (adoptive parents to adoptee)	I must hide my biological differences and conform to their expectations.	*Psalm 139:13-14* "For thou has possessed my reigns: thou hast covered me in my mother's womb. I will praise thee; for I am fearfully and wonderfully made..."	Differences are what make adoptive families unique. You contribute so much to our family.

Words that Hurt	How Adoptee May Translate	What God Says	Words that Heal
"Why would you want to open that can of worms?" (when adult adoptee expresses desire to search for birthmother.)	I must be unwise or maladjusted to wonder about my past.	*Exodus 4:27* *"And the Lord said to Aaron, Go into the wilderness to meet Moses. And he went and met him in the mount of God, and kissed him.*	It's very healthy to wonder about your birth family and history. It is a God-given need for many adoptees. It was for Moses, an adoptee who lived in Bible times.
"Let sleeping dogs lie." (In reference to searching for birth mother.)	I will be asking for trouble even to consider searching. My needs are not important.	*Isaiah 43:26* *"Put me in remembrance: let us plead together: declare thou, that thou mayest be justified.*	God often calls us to examine our past with Him so that we can live fully in the present.
"You don't need to search for your identity— you are "in Christ" - that's all you need to know."	I am not free to express my adoption needs to fellow Christians without being judged.	*Matthew 1:1, 17* *"The book of the generations of Jesus Christ, the Son of David .. So all the generations from Abraham to David are fourteen generations..."*	You have a right to know your biological history—Jesus did.

Words that Hurt	How Adoptee May Translate	What God Says	Words that Heal
"Do your adoptive parents know that you are searching?" (to an adult adoptee)	I am still a child. I can't make decisions without my parents' permission or approval.	*1 Corinthians 13:11* "When I was a child, I spake as a child, I understood as a child, I thought as a child: but when I begame a man, I put away childish things.*	I admire your courageous decision to search. Are your adoptive parents supportive?
"You were rejected by your birth family because you took control of your life back from God by going ahead with a reunion."	I am bad and my badness caused my family to reject me.	*John 1:11* "He came unto his own and his own received him not.*	I can't fathom the depth of the pain from your birth family's rejection. Jesus' own rejected Him also. He understands and is here for you. I am also.

-From *Jewel Among Jewels, Adoption News*, Winter 1996
Web: http://www.adoptionjewels.org
Email: mail@adoptionjewels.org

Appendix Number Five

Who Says You're Crazy?!

Is the whole world crazy? If psychologists are to be believed, it would seem so. In 1994 the American Psychological Association published a report which found that nearly half of the U.S. population has had a mental illness at some time.[1]

If half of the population is mentally ill, how can you be sure that you're not among them? The next time you are having conversation with another person, observe them closely. If they seem normal, you're it! Joking aside, many Americans sincerely believe that they are crazy.

There is no lack of voices to agree with them. Chief among these is the Diagnostical and Statistical Manual (DSM) of the American Psychiatric Association (APA).

The influence of this publication cannot be overstated. It is not only a weighty volume in its sheer size (over 800 pages in length and weighing in at almost three pounds), its power to shape public opinion is enormous. With its aura of academic respectability and scientific precision, and its wide audience, it is literally shaping the way Americans think. Paula Caplan was an insider in its formation and has first-hand knowledge of its influence. She writes, "…all trainees must learn [it] from cover to cover. It is also used as the key volume for a great deal of the research on mental health and mental illnesses funded by government agencies and private foundations."[2] Its influence doesn't stop there, however. "Insurance companies, general practitioners, and lawyers make frequent use of the manual, insurance companies to decide which patients to reimburse for their inpatient or outpatient treatments."[3]

It has been a runaway bestseller. Not only do libraries have to buy it but so do practicing therapists and mental health researchers. With 36 thousand psychiatrists in the U.S. along with 42 thousand clinical psychologists, 80 thousand clinical social workers, and 40 thousand marriage and family counselors, it should be no surprise that the last edition sold over 1.1 million copies! It is everywhere! It has literally become the "bible" of psychotherapy as we know it today!

Its popularity represents a frightening escalation of the labeling frenzy which began at the turn of the century. The official list of mental illnesses in 1880 numbered only seven. By 1917 that had grown to fifty nine. In the ensuing thirty years, the APA has published four editions of the DSM, each with more disorders than the last. The first edition of 1952 listed 106, the third included 297, and the most recent (DSM-IV) lists 486! Its anyone's guess what the next edition will hold.

Unfortunately, while posing as an encyclopedia of information, it is, in fact, a handbook of disinformation. It has spawned an entirely new vocabulary of psychospeak in our generation insuring that most people have at least a nodding acquaintance with such DSM conditions as "obsessive-compulsive disorder," "bi-polar disorder," "impulse-control disorder," and other "personality disorders."

I was visiting with a counselor friend and colleague some time ago when I noticed the frequent sprinkling of diagnostic labels in his conversation. When I asked about this, he excitedly pulled the DSM from his shelf to show me how informative it was in understanding his counselees. Like him, many Christians have bought into the practice of identifying people by a category of behavior provided by this secular publication.

Case Studies

They would be very interested in the case of one man I learned of who had a plethora of psychological maladies. The DSM diagnosis of this man is absolutely overwhelming! Even as he talked to his doctors, his Delusional Disorder/ Persecutorial Type was evident as he was convinced that the doctor was out to make him miserable. In claiming to be more than one person, he was seen as not only possessing a Multiple Personality Disorder but also a Dissociative Identity Disorder. He was tormented by Bi-Polar Disorder with terrible mood swings from manic hyperactivity to abject depression characterized by constant crying which resulted in a Sleep Disorder. His Conduct Disorder was clearly seen in that he attacked everyone he encountered; and to make matters worse, his tendency to Exhibitionism was evident in his propensity to walk about totally naked. In addition to these, he was diagnosed with Social Anxiety Disorder, Oppositional Defiant Disorder, Generalized Anxiety Disorder, Intermittent Explosive Disorder, and Schizoaffective Disorder, and others.

Complicating matters further, his attending physician was diagnosed with Delusional Disorder/Grandiose Type because he met the criteria listed in the DSM: "delusions of inflated worth, power, knowledge, identity or special relationship to a deity or famous person."

Perhaps by now, these men are sounding familiar to you. They should. The first is the maniac of Gadara as described in the Gospels. The second is none other than the Great Physician, our Lord Jesus Christ Himself. His contemporaries were so concerned about Him that they tried to restrain Him because they thought He was crazy! "[H]is friends...went out to lay hold on him: for they said, He is beside himself," (Mark 3:21) perhaps because He fit the classic description of the DSM label of Delusional Disorder. After all, He did claim to be God.

I confess that it was me and not a psychiatrist who assigned these labels, but the reader is invited to examine the criteria of these disorders for himself in the DSM-IV and see firsthand the accuracy of these designations.

Had modern psychiatrists and Christian psychologists used the DSM, they would have come to these same conclusions. They probably would have prescribed four to five years of intense therapy or even commitment to a mental institution. They also may have begun an intense pharmacological intervention program of drug therapy as well.

The Advantages of Labels

Giving the DSM authors the benefit of the doubt, we must concede that some few advantages are found in the practice of labeling. We will disclose the darker side of the DSM later, and there is plenty of darkness to go around, but for now, let's give the authors their due in seeking to bring some degree of help to mankind.

Welch suggests several advantages of using labels; relief in knowing there is a name for this problem, knowledge that others have experienced it and therefore I am not alone in this struggle, and the hope that a label gives the victim in suggesting that at least there is some knowledge available of what's happening to me, that one's struggle is recognizable by others. He suggests further that technical definitions as found in labels are, in fact, a "worthwhile attempt" to standardize the definition of the problem at hand.[4]

John Babler suggests an advantage for the counselor in having a working knowledge of the labels and the DSM and uses the example of an anorexic teen: "If a young girl and her parents come in for counseling because they have tried the "psychological" approach and it did not work, you can be sure they know all the DSM-IV criteria for the condition of anorexia. So I not only need to know those criteria myself, but I must be able to think and respond biblically, even at our initial meeting."[5] A counselor familiar with the DSM would also have a natural point of contact from which to lead her secular thinking into biblical understanding.

The Dangers of Labels

At the same time, let's remember that the DSM practice of labeling is misguided, as seen in the consequences of this dangerous practice. The foolishness of setting up a system of comparative labels is clear; "For we dare not... compare ourselves with some that commend themselves: but they, measuring themselves by themselves, and comparing themselves among themselves, are not wise." (2 Corinthians 10:12) Exactly how this is not wise is clearly seen.

Avoiding Personal Responsibility

Chief among the dangers of labeling is the unavoidable conclusion that sinful behavior is not the fault of the sinner; after all, he couldn't help himself. In his book The Abuse Excuse, Harvard law professor Alan Dershowitz lists 52 excuses used in court to avoid punishment. The most famous is the "Twinkie Defense" used by a man who committed a double murder and blamed it on the influence of the junk food he was consuming. The jury accepted his

argument. Other notable excuses include the Battered Wife
Syndrome, the Black Rage Defense, Chronic Lateness
Syndrome, Multiple Personality Disorder, the Pornography
Defense for rape offenses, Repressed Memory Syndrome,
and even the Unhappy Gay Sailor Syndrome.[6]

One category in the DSM exchanges the outmoded
designation of "drunkenness" for which a man was once held
responsible, for the more fashionable Substance-Induced
"disorder." Such a prestigious inclusion in the DSM
automatically implies victimization, grants respectability, and
even insures financial remuneration for treatment from most
insurance companies.

Were it not so tragic, this victimization of America
would be laughable. In fact, when some of these disorders
are first introduced, they are laughed at. Then the
combination of the weight of science falsely-so-called, the
pressure of political correctness, and the appeal of an
acceptable scapegoat come to bear on the bemused. The
critic is then often intimidated into silence or accepts the
party line. Rejecting a sense of personal responsibility
becomes positively trendy. The unavoidable result of this is
that in time it leads to a pervasive mentality of victimization.

The "Victim" Mentality

A popular refrain in our age is "I can't help it! It's
not my fault!" A passive victim mentality has insulated all
sinners from any conviction over their sins, and the labeling
craze bears much of the blame. We have reduced sinful

actions to a mere reaction to unfair treatment where we can't be held responsible for our reactions of anger. We come from dysfunctional homes and are therefore dysfunctional. If abuse, abandonment, or molestation is in our pasts, we are excused from normalcy and above all victory, because of its irreversible effects on our lives. In short, we are no longer sinners who are responsible for our choices and actions, we are victims who blame others for our inability to succeed.

Once the victim mindset is embraced, it is but a small step to a permanent way of thinking. Bulkley writes, "A… major problem with psycholabels is perpetual victimization. When one accepts his label, he is forever categorized."[7]

The value of a good name cannot be overstated. "A good name is rather to be chosen than great riches, and loving favour rather than silver and gold." (Proverbs 22:1). Giving a person a good name is to give him a positive expectation. This is why it is important for parents to exercise care in choosing a name for their child. We tend to rise or fall according to the expectations of others, and a name is the expression of that expectation.

In like manner, to give a person a bad expectation via a bad name or label is to court disaster. There is a saying in East Tennessee, "Give a dog a bad name and he'll kill himself living up to it." Telling a child he is stupid is dangerous for this reason. Likewise, labeling him deficient is dangerous for the same reason. The DSM represents a sophisticated expression of such labeling.

There is also the ever present danger of self-fulfilling

prophecies. Once a person is labeled mentally ill, he is more inclined to act that way. As Jay Adams writes, "...there is always the danger that some persons who have been inaccurately labeled will try to live up to the label. This can happen when one is looking for an excuse to get out of work or to justify his sinful behavior; or...the label shapes the person's life as he closes out options that the label doesn't allow him to enter."[8]

The victimization of the labeled person often results in the opposite response. If not defeated by his label, he may overreact to it to prove himself otherwise. Adams warns, "they may try to live it down (spend unnecessary time and energy denying it).[9]

Strangely, many sincere Christians have unreservedly embraced this victim mentality. They seem to base it on misapplied Scriptures such as Exodus 20:5-6 which refers to the "iniquity of the fathers" being passed on to the children, and Proverbs 22:6 which is interpreted as meaning that a parent determines the conduct of the child, both of which bear careful scrutiny and exegesis before making such psychological evaluations. A study of Ezekiel 18 is the best cure for this. (See the "Sour Grapes" section of this book.)

Confusion

To say that psycholabeling causes confusion is an understatement. The first result of this is to cause the labeled person to view themselves as sick rather than seeing their feelings or actions as sinful. This is a classic ploy of the enemy. Confusing our actions with our personhood is a tried and proven method of discouraging the spirit and paralyzing the will. He has always delighted in blurring the distinction between acts of sin and the state of sin. God takes the opposite tack. He addresses the act of sin. For example, God says "You told a lie," while Satan says "You're a liar!" God says "You committed robbery" while Satan says "You're a robber." One addresses the actions while the other accuses the person. Sadly, the DSM accuses as well. Such confusion leads to defeatism.

Another result of the confusion is the tendency to focus on the label itself instead of the individual criteria needed to establish the label. The result is a misdirected focus for treatment. As Caplan writes, "What may actually be fairly ordinary feelings and behavior are then renamed signs of mental disorder so that often no one responds to these emotions and behavior themselves but instead treats them as signs of the construct called mental disorder, so they switch the focus to the presumed problem."[10] This results in ignoring the parts for the whole. Babler explains, "The core thesis of the DSM-IV is that there is a whole greater than the sum of the parts, a "diagnosis" that explains the "symptoms." For example, if you exhibit, say, six or more typical behaviors, emotions, and mental processes (the parts) over a six-month period, you qualify to receive one big diagnostic label (the whole.) The label identifies the "disorder" that you have or embody."[11]

Ignoring the parts of the whole for the label itself results in a grossly misdirected therapy, for better to treat the individual symptoms as a target of change in themselves. This approach is within the reach of all and certainly the biblical way to lead someone into change. Babler agrees, "… each of the typical behaviors, emotions, and mental processes (the parts) is addressed by the Bible, without attaching a pseudo-scientific label as a supposed whole. Scripture does not speak about "obsessive-compulsive disorder" as a whole diagnosis, but the Lord does relevantly and directly counsel someone who exhibits each of the behaviors that qualify one for such a behavior."[12] For example, the DSM criteria for Oppositional Defiant Disorder (ODD) is "a pattern of negativistic, hostile and defiant behavior lasting at least six months during which four or more of the following are present: often loses temper, argues with adults, often actively defies or refuses to comply with adults' requests or rules, often deliberately annoys people, often blames others for his or her mistakes, is often touchy or easily annoyed by others." Looking at ODD as a medicalized disorder takes the responsibility off the counselee and locks them into a mindset which justifies and encourages sin. "Clearly, the DSM takes the focus off of sin and ends up being a manual about how to be a victim of syndromes and disorders."[13]

On the other hand, to take each of the criteria and treat them biblically not only gives tools for change but conveys hope. It makes the counselee responsible for his actions. Ceasing from anger (Psalm 37:8) and being obedient to parents (Colossians 3:20) addresses the individual sins in the DSM list and gives hope for victory. Labeling a person into a category destroy hope.

Loss of Hope

This vacuum of hope is the direct result of misdiagnosis, misdirected therapy and excusing of sin. Although psychology and psychiatry are strong in describing the problem, they fail miserably in explaining it, and therefore cannot offer a viable solution. As proof of their ability to describe the problem, one can merely glance at the DSM; page after page describes the emotions, the actions, and the thought processes. This is their strength. But describing a problem by no means guarantees the ability to explain it let alone solve it. Many people can describe a tornado and its aftereffects while being clueless about how to rebuild the city.

The biblical counselor, on the other hand, can take the counselee to the next level. He can explain the problem. That's because the Bible has the explanation. While counseling a couple struggling with chronic arguing who had spent thousand of dollars on psychotherapy to no avail, I told them, "I know what the problem is." In shocked disbelief they asked, "How can you know what the problem is in only one session!? We have been in therapy for months and nobody could help us!" I had them read aloud Proverbs 13:10 "Only by pride cometh contention."

Once an explanation is in hand, there is hope. The same Bible that explains the problem gives a cure for it. Adams recalls one counselee "who was describing a problem he said he somehow couldn't put his finger on. After listening for a while I said, "Why, what you've been describing to me is jut plain, old-fashioned pride!" Instantly, his eyes lit up and he shouted, "Ah! That's it! Now that I have a name for it, I know what I must do about it!" Adams concludes, "The label enabled him to get a grasp of the problem and pointed to its solution."[14] Pointing to the solution is the natural goal of biblical counseling which understands the spiritual nature of man. Labeling is merely a description without a biblical explanation or solution.

Conclusion

The Christian must never allow psychotherapy to define the terms. It is time for biblical counselors to stop playing by psychology's rules! Rather than allowing the practice of psychospeak to draw us away from the Bible, we must judge the labels by the Scriptures. By forcing psychological language to conform to biblical language, we now have an explanation which leads to a biblical solution. It is not phobia, it's fear. It is not ODD, it's rebellion. It is not Substance Abuse Disorder, it's drunkenness. It is not Bi-Polar Disorder, it is a mood swing or loss of self control or temperance. Labels describe the problems, but don't explain them. If they can't explain them, they certainly can't cure them. Biblical counseling does both.

Unlike the labeling game which locks a person into a perpetual inescapable category of "disorder" and makes them dependent on therapy and drugs to merely sustain some degree of normalcy, biblical counseling gives hope! This hope comes from identifying the problem biblically and giving a biblical solution. Something that any Christian with a modicum of biblical knowledge can do.

Carol Tavris, in recommending Caplan's book wrote, "Mental health professionals need to read this book to cure themselves of 'Delusional Scientific Diagnosing Disorder' and the public needs to read it for self protection." The same recommendation can be given for the Word of God. It is the cure.

It's Not My Fault!

I went to my psychiatrist to be psychoanalyzed;
To find out why I killed my cat and blackened my wife's
eyes.

He put me on a downy couch to see what he could find;
And this is what he dredged up from my subconscious mind.

When I was one, my mommy hid my dolly in the trunk;
And so it follows naturally that I am always drunk.

When I was two, I saw my father kiss the maid one day;
And that is why I suffer now from kleptomania.

When I was three, I suffered from ambivalence toward my
brothers;
And so it follows naturally, I poisoned all my lovers.

Appendix Number Six

The Biblical Path to Lasting Change

Where are all our converts?! Why do so few who claim salvation show a change in their lives? Why do so few who change really stick? Why do so few who stick really seem to make a difference? The answer to these timeless questions may be found in a failure to follow God's plan for lasting change. " But God be thanked, that ye were the servants of sin, but ye have obeyed from the heart that form of doctrine which was delivered you." (Romans 6:17) Throughout Romans chapter six Paul makes a compelling case for a distinct change in the three basic parts of man's personality; the mind, the heart, and the will. In this single verse he summarizes his teaching. He commends the Roman Christians for changing at all three levels: the will; "Ye have obeyed," the heart; "from the heart," the mind; "that form of doctrine." Lasting spiritual change must address and impact all three.

God always addresses truth to the conscious mind of man, his intellectual part. From there it affects the heart. The heart in Scriptures represents both the emotions and the convictions of a man. After the heart is changed a man is compelled to action; "Ye have obeyed <u>from the heart</u>," That action is the result of the will being changed.

So the path of life-changing truth always follows a predictable course; from the head to the heart to the hand. First, you learn it, then you love it, and then you live it. Consider the chart below.

"Doctrine"	Intellectual	Head	Learn It
▼ "Heart"	▼ Emotional / Convictional	▼ Heart	▼ Love It
▼ "Obeyed"	▼ Volitional	▼ Hand	▼ Live It

To skip a step or focus inordinately on only one of them will deceive the seeker, and distract him from lasting victory. And yet these are the common approaches to much counseling and discipleship. We choose a cold, academic approach with the notion that truth alone is the solution, or we skip the "doctrine" stage and go right for the heart, in hopes of an emotional experience. The aggressive counselor may even attempt to force his own convictions upon the heart of the follower. The more self-sufficient seeker may be attracted to the purely volitional level of conquering via the power of the will alone. Each of thee approaches may have a temporary effect, but none of them alone can bring lasting spiritual victory.

Isaiah warns of the danger of incomplete change. " . . . *Forasmuch as this people draw near me with their mouth (will), and with their lips do honour me (will), but have removed their heart far from me (heart), and their fear toward me is taught by the precept of men (mind)." (Isaiah 29:13)* This is a picture of a busy-handed, empty-hearted, full-headed believer living in defeat.

Though it is not wrong at some point to address the heart or will directly, it is ineffective if not dangerous to do so while ignoring the mind. The beginning place of lasting change is in the "doctrine" or truths which change the rest of man.

". . . [Y]e shall know the truth, and the truth shall [set] you free." (John 8:38).

I have heard many people plead, "Help me to feel better," or "Show me how I can stop sinning," but I have yet to hear someone ask, "Help me to change my belief system," and yet effective counseling begins with the mind where the counselee is enabled to put off the lies and put on the truth.

A crowd gathered to watch the victim of a tragic accident lying face down in a growing pool of blood. One man lit a cigarette while nonchalantly leaning against the guard rail. "Somebody should help that guy before he bleeds to death," he casually intoned. The paramedics arrived and turned the victim over. The man with the cigarette threw it down and screamed, "Oh my soul! Somebody do something! That's my brother!" The truth had moved from the head which stirred the heart and changed the life.

A changed life is always the result of "Obey[ing] from the heart that form of doctrine." (Romans 6:17)

Appendix Number Seven

Adoption and Fetal Alcohol Syndrome

Fetal Alcohol Syndrome is "the leading cause
of mental retardation in the western world."

Dr. Edward Riley
Chairman, U.S. National Task Force
on FAS/FAE
December 4, 2000

A major argument in favor of open adoption (open access to the background of the adoptive child; especially his medical records) is the belief that in understanding the child and insuring complete medical protection, the adoptive parent must have a comprehensive grasp of his physical and biological make-up, including any potential diseases inherited from one of his biological parents.

While it is clear that many physical maladies can originate with the parents' genetic and biological make-up, it is not as clearly understood that brain damage and resultant mental abnormalities can also originate with the mother who indulges in alcohol while carrying the child.

Unfortunately, the first trimester of pregnancy is the most important, as this is the time when the formation of the brain is most sensitive to exposure to alcohol. This is also the very time when the birth mother can be the most unaware of her pregnancy. Ingestion of alcohol during this time can create permanent and irreversible brain damage lasting into childhood. It is not known precisely how much alcohol is consumed or how often. Evidence indicates the smallest amount can have an effect. The mother may have a hangover for a day, but the child has one for a lifetime.

Our son Jonathan was the unknowing victim of this malady, discovered only after he had reached adulthood and his birth mother, prior to her suicide, confessed to drinking heavily in an effort to abort him. Subsequent evaluations by a leading national expert on Fetal Alcohol Syndrome (FAS) revealed the worst case ever brought to her attention.

A primary dysfunction brought on by FAS is impulsivity with little regard for consequences. An FAS child lives for the moment with little capacity to anticipate the future.

Because a major pool of adoptive children is from unwed mothers living in sinful lifestyles and foreign babies exposed to rampant parental alcoholism, the adoptive parent is well advised to understand this serious condition and its lesser cousin, Fetal Alcohol Effect (FAE).

FAS/FAE typically goes unnoticed and undiagnosed. The knowledge of this condition in the United States is far behind our northern neighbor, Canada, where they have been forced to deal with this due to the high population of native Indians and their attendant high rate of alcoholism.

We were unaware of our own son's diagnosis until a wise pastor's wife suggested that he might have FAS and recommended the book **Fantastic Antone Succeeds**. When we read it, we realized the truth, but the full scope of his condition did not come out until his capital trial when an FAS expert testified on his behalf.

Effects of FAS/FAE

Fetal Alcohol Syndrome is "The Leading Cause of Mental Retardation in the Western World"

60% experience legal trouble (in trouble with authorities, charged with a crime, convicted of a crime)

14% - ages 6-11

61% - adolescents

58% - adults

95% have mental health problems

62% have difficulties in school

50% end up being confined (75% of men)

"FAS may be the single most pervasive factor leading to crime".

52% engage in inappropriate sexual behavior

30% struggle with substance abuse

80% cannot live alone

80% have trouble with employment, including keeping a job

69% have biological mother who is dead

16% are diagnosed with Antisocial Personality Disorder

7,000-10,000 born with it yearly

Other Symptoms of FAS/FAE

Delay of growth in prenatal and postnatal stages of life

Cranio-facial anomalies

Central nervous system impairments

Poor judgment

Behavioral problems

Attention problems

Social struggles

Poor adaptive functioning

Difficulty handling money

Conclusion

Because of the probability of a connection between FAS/FAE and adoptive children, the adoptive parent is well advised to make a thorough examination of the possibility of FAS in their own child. The presence of such a diagnosis could indicate the need of a modified approach in parenting styles to fit the limitations of the child. While doing this, however, the emphasis of personal responsibility must be kept before the child at all times. FAS is an influence, and a major one as well, but must not be allowed to become an excuse for misbehavior.

At the same time, never forget that "The king's heart is in the hand of the Lord; as the rivers of water, he turneth it whitersoever he will. (Proverbs 21:1). No matter what the special needs of a child may be, our loving heavenly Father watches over them. It is to Him that our appeals must be made and our trust focused. Our son has shown significant spiritual progress of late, for which we are greatly encouraged. We can only praise God for bringing him to this point.

Appendix Number Eight

Does A Prodigal Child Disqualify a Man From the Pastoral Ministry?

An evangelist is accused of unfitness for ministry because his teenage daughter has committed immorality. A missionary is recalled because his daughter is rebellious and he is therefore deemed "disqualified" for ministry. A pastor is asked for his resignation because his teenage son stole from the local department store. Three potential leaders on the verge of losing their life's ministry because, they are told, their failure as parents has rendered them unfit for spiritual leadership.

The fallout from such conclusions is devastating the church. Pastors and wives become discouraged as marriages are brought under pressure in efforts to produce the "perfect" child. Parents of good children judge other parents while those with wayward children assume horrendous burdens of guilt. Children of leaders chafe under the demands of their fishbowl existence and resent the ministry for its unyielding demands upon them. Christians at large unleash barbs of criticism against hurting leaders. Pressure is brought to bear for resignations, and indeed many conscientious spiritual leaders do resign their positions and leave the full-time gospel ministry.

Few questions have plagued the church like the one swirling around the issue of leadership qualification, specifically in I Timothy 3:1-7, and Titus 1:6-9, and few of these have been more misused than the ones related to the leader and his children.

REASONS FOR CONFUSION

Determinism

The reasons for this dilemma vary, but topping the list is the church's infatuation with the belief of determinism. We have believed Freud's lie that a child's life is determined primarily, if not exclusively, by the training of the parent. We have taken this teaching into our churches, dressed it hastily in the garb of "biblical teaching" and taught a generation or two that the parent is solely responsible for the behavior of the child. For many, Proverbs 22:6 has become an icon in the church and an idol of the heart. But this passage is no more an absolute promise than is *Proverbs 15:1, "A soft answer turneth away wrath.... "* Generally speaking, it's true that a soft answer will defuse a hot temper, but every time?! And generally speaking, if a child is trained up ". . . in the way he should go": and when he is old, he will not depart from it." But always?" Ezekiel chapter 18 corrects this myth as do the words of our own Heavenly Father about His children Israel, *"... I have (nurtured) and brought up children, and they have rebelled against me." (Isaiah 1:2).* Christian leaders are under enormous pressure to rear "perfect" children because of being "spoiled" by the philosophy of determinism.

Fear of Man

Then there is the ever present and pervasive "fear of man." If ever it were true that *"The fear of man bringeth a snare," (Proverbs 29:25)*, it is true in the role of spiritual leaders and their children. As much as we deplore the "political correctness" of the world, we practice it in the church. We make the opinion of Christian educators, leading pastors, and mission heads the litmus test of this belief. As one pastor said to me when I asked him why he believed a leader was disqualified by a rebellious child, "That's what they taught me in Bible college."

The fear of man is a double-sided coin; one side is the need of acceptance, the other side is the fear of rejection. When we form our beliefs from the teachings of men and have never *"...searched the scriptures daily, whether those things (are) so," (Acts 17:11),* it is often because we are motivated by the fear of man. When we consider resignation based on popular opinion or because of what the "brethren" might say, we are victims of the fear of man. The important issue is God's opinion not man's! *"The fear of the Lord is the beginning of wisdom..." (Psalm 111:10).*

Spiritual Warfare

Another reason, often overlooked, is the attack of the enemy himself. He is called the *"accuser of our brethren" in Revelation 12:10.* "Accuser" comes from the Greek word "KATEGOROS" from which we derive the word "category." The devil loves nothing more than to defeat the brethren by categorizing them into a classification of "failure" or "unfit." But we know that he is the father of lies. We need to exercise extreme caution before we give him heed.

And what of the danger to our children when we make them the criteria of our fitness for ministry? If the devil *"as a roaring lion, walketh about, seeking whom he may devour," (1 Peter 5:8)* won't he, like any lion, target the feeble, the weak, and the young first? Have we set our children up for his attack by basing the strength of our calling on the weakest of our family?

Questioning the Messenger

It is assumed by many proponents of the "unfit by virtue of a prodigal child" viewpoint that any argument for mercy and leniency is automatically suspect if the children of the proponent have gone astray. How can any pastor whose children were ever prodigal be trusted to bring objectivity to the table? As one leader wrote to me, "I am fearful that because of the number of men in the ministry, especially those we would consider leaders, have failed with the raising of their children, we will water down God's stand on the issue." A Christian publication writes, "it is regrettable but true that [these men] . . have either lost their children or are in the process of doing so." These men represent a common argument used against pastors with wayward children. They seem to say, "The truth is tempered by the situation from which it arises." To the degree that any teacher speaks out of disappointment, his teaching is untrustworthy. By casting aspersions on the messenger, the message is negated and by what greater aspersion than corrupted motives.

To conclude that a message is disqualified because of the messenger's pain-motivation is to impugn the very heart of ministry. The Scriptures are clear that suffering can be a qualifier rather than a disqualifier for the promulgation of truth. A soul winner who was lost in sin is motivated to warn others about its dangers. A counselor who failed in some area of his life is compelled to help others avoid that pitfall. A pastor who has lived with the excruciating pain of despair over a sinful child is moved to help a brother pastor avoid the snare which almost destroyed him.

If we "... comfort . . . by the comfort wherewith we ourselves are comforted of God." (2 Corinthians 1:4), does this not assume a burden which required comfort in the first place? And if being comforted is a primary qualification for comforting, perhaps the humbled parent of a wayward child is better positioned than others to minister in this needy area.

I have been attacked in two national periodicals for taking a stand for mercy in this area, even being accused of "blasphemy" and of "trying to destroy the faith of many." (In neither case was I contacted by my accusers.) This is not a subject which can be resolved by inflammatory rhetoric, name calling, or motive judging. Too much is at stake.

RE-EXAMINING THE ISSUE

A careful re-examination of the Scriptures is in order. While there is certainly a need to establish high standards of conduct for the pastor, the passages at hand may have been overused for this purpose.

Pre-Ordination Qualifications or Post-Ordination Requirements?

Although the Scriptures under consideration may not be intended exclusively for use before the pastor's call, the context indicates that this is the writer's primary intention. It is clear that his emphasis in these scriptures is to establish sound qualifications before enlistment or endorsement. The passage in I Timothy 3 begins with, ". . . If a man desire the office of a bishop, he desireth a good work," followed immediately with the qualifications of the office. The context indicates that the qualifications are for the volunteer to consider before seeking the office. The passage in Titus chapter 1 bears out the same meaning. Before the qualifications are listed, Paul clearly instructs Titus to ". . . ordain elders in every city, as I had appointed thee;" (Titus

1:5) then follows immediately with the qualification of the elders he should seek to appoint. On the one hand, the seeker of the office is faced with necessary qualifications. On the other hand, the appointer of men to the office is provided with qualifications to look for. In each case the emphasis is on qualifying the leader before ordination rather than after.

It certainly makes sense that before a man is ordained, he should meet some minimal standards as his adherence to them is some indication of his maturity as well as his ability to maintain them. But to extrapolate them into the future as inviolable requirements doesn't make sense. To be " blameless, of good behavior, patient, not self-willed, not soon angry, temperate, and have faithful children (meaning "believing children" or "children who believe") before ordination does not guarantee that these qualities will be perfectly and perpetually adhered to after ordination. What if the elder is blamed for something? What if his behavior is not always "good"? What if he loses his patience or worse his temper? What if he is not always temperate or self-controlled? Which failure in any of these areas disqualifies a man? Who determines whether it's a serious enough offense? Long enough in duration? Public enough in view? Who's to say that sin or failure in these areas cannot be confessed, forsaken and forgiven?

Hiring a Staff Member

Before hiring a man to work on your church staff you will review his resume, check his references and scrutinize his work record. Why? You want to take every precaution to insure that the man is qualified for the position. But once he is hired, if he fails in his responsibility, do you fire him outright? No, you correct him; and if he responds, you work with him. But the initial scrutiny of his character is essential before hiring him. In like manner, the pastor's pre-ministry character is in question in these passages. To assume, however, that pre-ordination qualifications equal post-ordination requirements is stretching the point.

Re-Thinking Ordination

In many ordinations, this process is reversed. I have sat on many ordination councils and heard few, if any, questions about the marriage of the candidate, his morals, or his children. But questions abound about his knowledge, philosophy, methodology, and doctrinal persuasion. Why is so little attention paid to a man's character before ordaining him , and so much emphasis placed on it afterwards? Maybe we need to "accuse the brethren" less after the fact and examine them more before.

Examining Prospective Church Members

When people present themselves for church membership, we examine them carefully and once assured of the genuineness of their conversion, we accept them into the church family. But does that examination guarantee a sinless life after they join the church? And what if they do sin? We confront them in love and discipline them if necessary even to the point of excommunication in an extreme case. Why?

To restore them.

As the goal with the church employee and the church member is to restore them, so should the goal be to the pastor's child who might have failed, as well as his disheartened father. Rod Bell writes of a missionary whose daughter rebelled.

"He had to leave the mission board because [they] asked him to come home since his family was not in subjection to him. They said he had disqualified himself from the ministry. I told him to be patient and love her with tough love and work through the situation. He certainly was on top of the situation, a good disciplinarian, and not only that, but a tender and compassionate man. He stayed on the field, left the mission board, and went out under our church. I counseled him weekly by phone and letters. God gave his daughter the victory. She is now 18 years old, and God has called her to the mission field. While a man must realize he has a holy obligation to have his family under subjection, there is not a family on the face of God's earth that does not go through some trials with teenagers. Therefore, we must treat our children as God treats His children. I am glad at God does not punish us, but chastens us when we do wrong.

Ruling Well

Thorough exegesis is also required when we look at the reason for the qualifications. Paul explains his reasoning to Timothy, "One that ruleth well his own house, having his children in subjection with all gravity; For if a man know not how to rule his own house, how shall he take care of the church of God?" (I Timothy 3:4-5). It is to be understood that initially, it is the quality of the leadership in question here, not the perfection of the follower. It is the responsibility of the father and pastor which is under consideration, not the response of the church member and child. The judgment as to whether a pastor is ruling well or not is not in the misbehavior of the church member but in the response of the leader to that misbehavior. If the pastor confronts the sin lovingly, and deals with it thoroughly and biblically, he has ruled well. In like manner, if the father confronts the sin of his children lovingly, and deals with it thoroughly and biblically, he has also ruled well. If pastors are not asked to resign over a wayward member if they have handled the situation properly, neither should they be asked to resign over a wayward child if they have handled the situation properly.

Ruling well certainly includes discipline, but the need of discipline indicates that there is a misbehavior in the first place. To require discipline from leaders on the one hand, and to assume the absence of misbehavior on the other is inconsistent. It is not the absence of misbehavior that qualifies a man for leadership, but his handling of it.

John Vaughn elaborates: "What does it mean to 'rule well'? Is this a man who has no disobedient member in his congregation? If one of them requires discipline, is he disqualified? To 'rule well' means to 'stand in front and lead,' to set an example (as an elder) of the truth he is preaching (as a bishop). To assume that a man seeking the office is permanently unqualified, or that a man in the office is automatically disqualified by the disobedience of his child is not illustrated in the many examples of Old Testament leaders whose sons were disobedient. Even the example of Eli teaches that the failure for which he was removed from the priesthood (by death) was that 'his sons made themselves vile, and **he restrained them not**' (emphasis added)."

There is a clear bilateral link between management in the family and management in the church. The home is the proving ground for leadership skills needed in the church. The requirements of the church mirror the requirements of the home. The church's response to the pastor's home leadership should parallel its response to his church leadership. The same standard for determining if the leader is ruling well in one should apply to the other as well.

Honest Re-Evaluation May Be Needed

At some point, of course, a general pervasiveness of disobedience may indicate a lack of   gifts, an inability to lead, or an absence of spirituality. This will be revealed first in the home. It is arguable that if five out of five children are publicly insubordinate, disobedient, ungodly, and accused of unrestrained sinfulness, the leader's credentials may require a renewed scrutiny. Bob Jones III comments:

> If a preacher has a household of children who are rotten, rebellious, or lewd and dissolute, he is unqualified to preach. I'm not sure, however, if one child goes astray and the others turn out well that a preacher is disqualified. . . . I think that we're unscripturally hard on Christian fathers in ministry when one child goes bad. We don't take into account the perfidy of the devil. It is possible for a child to go bad in spite of the best parenting and the best examples from father and mother. Each child is a free moral agent. Adam and Eve were God's children, and they exercised their free moral choice against God and for sin in a prefect moral environment.

A Uniform Code of Church Justice?

Who is qualified to say when a pastor is actually "unfit" because of his children's misbehavior? Obviously that decision must rest upon the conscience of the pastor and the decision of the church body. It should be bathed in earnest prayer, diligent study of the Word, and godly counsel. As in much of the Christian life, the issues are not black and white. A "letter of the law" approach will not work here. There are too many considerations, too many variables. Each situation must be weighed in the balances rather than attempting to establish a uniform code of church justice. As Bell says,

"I think each circumstance should be judged on the effectiveness and diligence with which the pastor deals with his family . . . in each circumstance, everything must be judged upon its own merit."

Conclusion

Who is better qualified to do this than the local autonomous body of believers? The ultimate responsibility of sorting through all the issues in making a decision regarding the pastor's fitness rests upon the local church.

There is an unsettling inconsistency in the church today. While many pastors deplore any challenge to the "independent" nature of the local, autonomous church, some of them feel no compunctions about passing judgment on another brother or a sister church in this matter of a pastor's wayward children. If we truly believe in the self governing status of the church, each assembly must be given the liberty to determine their own destiny.

The burden of proof is upon the person who is challenging a pastor's fitness to lead based on his children's misbehavior. Dare anyone take a casual approach to this? Cavalier conclusions and hasty judgments must be brought to the Word of God for final disposition. Any decision, generalized or specific, to disqualify a leader based on his child's waywardness demands that the accuser be fully and scripturally persuaded in his own mind. Are you?

Appendix Number Nine

Can Church Members Go to Hell?

When I first became a Christian, I assumed that all church going people were automatically qualified for the fast track into Heaven. It was a given. After becoming a church member, then a pastor, I had to rethink the issue. Following a careful study of the Bible, my thinking has been drastically changed.

When I began this counseling ministry several years ago, I assumed that all pastors and church leaders were on their way to Heaven as well. After counseling over 600 pastors, missionaries, evangelists, and wives, my thinking has again been drastically changed.

I remember well the consternation I felt when one pastor's wife boldly began a counseling session with these words: "Brother Binney, something is bothering me about your counseling!" Well, that got my attention. "What is it?" I asked. "We have been here for two days and you haven't even asked us if we are Christians!" She was right. And the reason I had not was because I naively assumed they were already Christians.

Since then I have encountered many leaders who doubted their faith, others who could not clearly explain how they were saved, and even others who frankly admitted that they had never even been saved. Imagine 20 pastors confessing their lost condition in one city! It happened. In the book The Light and the Glory, its authors record that when George Whitefield preached in Boston, 20 of its prominent preachers admitted they were unsaved and trusted Christ for salvation. Dr. Bob Jones Sr. would not be shocked by such knowledge. In his booklet What is a Christian, he said, "I have spent nearly my entire life in association with ministers…nobody would tell you that every preacher in American is a saved man."

As I examine the testimonies of such church leaders in counseling and evaluated their stumbling explanation of how a person obtains salvation, I realized that the church is facing a major dilemma. Not only do these leaders not see the issues clearly for themselves, they are passing on a legacy of confusion to their followers and converts. "If the blind lead the blind, both shall fall into the ditch." (Matthew 15:14). I was soon to learn that this ditch was more akin to a cavernous valley!

As this awareness began to grow, two books came into my hands that crystallized my thinking. They were The Almost Christian Discovered written in 1661 by a godly Puritan pastor named Matthew Mead, and Preaching to A Dying Nation by Dr. R.L. Hymers and Dr. Christopher Cagan of Los Angeles, California. In a bold frontal attack on the state of the church and its insipid spirituality, the authors of these books argue persuasively for the need of a purified membership in the church. I recommend them to the reader but warn you that you had better read them only after buckling your seat belt, donning a crash helmet, and calling your insurance company! They are not for the squeamish at heart.

God was doing His work in my heart. His truth was following its course in my thinking in the predictable progressive way of much enlightenment. From a denial of any problems to unsettling doubt about the presumed normalcy of things, God led me into the discovery of truth. Then I was confronted with a sense of duty about my role in addressing this need and finally a devotion was born in my heart to make a difference. Thus, the reason for this writing.

My conclusion is that it is not only possible for religious people to go to hell, they are rushing there by the droves! I am not merely referring to the religious of the cults we so deplore, nor even the religious from dead, mainline denominations which have grown cold and liberal in their theology. I am referring to the religious of the right-wing, militant, separated, fundamental, world-shunning, Bible-believing churches as well.

I realize the controversy and even confusion of such a position. The very idea that clean-cut, church-going, morally upright people could go to hell sounds preposterous. But I take the chance of being misunderstood because so much is at stake.

Here are some of the reasons I have come to this conclusion.

Christ Taught It

In Matthew's Gospel, chapter seven, the Lord Jesus Christ clearly states that many good people will go to hell. He is addressing some of the most moral, actively religious people of history; and yet He warns them to "Enter ye in at the strait gate: for wide is the gate, and broad is the way, that leadeth to destruction, and many there be which go in thereat: Because strait is the gate, and narrow is the way, which leadeth unto life, and few there be that find it." (Matthew 7:13-14) Jesus says that there is a tiny gate with a narrow path which leads to Heaven and few ever find it ... even few of the religious! At the same time, there is a very wide gate and a broad thoroughfare crowded with religious people who are headed to destruction.

Jesus knew there were people listening to His words who sincerely prayed to God. They had prayed for their salvation and prayed earnestly and sincerely. He had to confront them, however, with the vanity of their prayers; "Not every one that saith unto me, Lord, Lord, shall enter into the kingdom of heaven; but he that doeth the will of my Father which is in heaven." (Matthew 7:21)

Of course, He knew there would be a howl of protests from the law-keepers and the religious devotees. "But Lord, don't we serve you!? Don't we peach for you and devote ourselves to good works!? How can you say we are headed for destruction!?" Before they could give voice to their protests, Jesus cut them off. "Many will say to me in that day, Lord, Lord, have we not prophesied in thy name? and in thy name have cast out devils? and in thy name done many wonderful works?"(v. 22).

Note here what these religious people were relying on for their salvation: their witnessing, the wonders they performed, and the good works they did. Some were saying, "But I teach the Bible, sing in the choir, even evangelize the neighborhood. Doesn't that count?" Others were claiming that their power to exorcise demons qualified them as uniquely spiritual and heaven-bound. Still others resorted to the old stand-by of good works. "We feed the hungry, clothe the poor, help our neighbors and serve our church! We are of all people bound for heaven! Right?" "Wrong," said Jesus, and for good reason. One essential qualification was missing; their claims did not meet the "will of the Father." The person who attains salvation is the one "that doeth the will of my Father which is in heaven." They insisted that they were doing God's will, even going so far as to say it was all "in thy name."

The meaning of this little phrase "in thy name" is largely misunderstood and misapplied in our Christian culture of today. To pray "in Jesus' name" implies that it is done according to His will and direction. This prayer is according to the will of God, thus the power of Christ's promise, "If ye shall ask anything in my name, I will do it." (John 14:14). To invoke Jesus' name also means that because it is His will, all His authority stands behind it. When a policeman knocks on the door of a suspect's home and declares, "Open up in the name of the law!" he is saying that not only has the state sent him, but all the power and authority of the state is behind him! This is heavy-duty stuff, so much so that to don a policeman's uniform or to misrepresent his authority is a violation of the law. It is no light thing.

And it is no light thing when a man insists his soul's eternal destiny rests on a church-mandated or religiously-inspired mantra of man's making. Using Jesus' name for our claim to salvation when Jesus neither willed it or authorized it merely serves to compound the sin. This is clear from the scathing response of Christ, "I never knew you: depart from me, ye that work iniquity." (Matthew 7:23).

In one fell swoop Christ tore out the underpinnings of their false faith; their alleged knowledge of God; "I never knew you," their assumed proximity to God; "depart from me," and the presumed righteousness of their numerous "wonderful works" for God; "ye that work iniquity."

And why shouldn't our Lord respond in this way! The Heavenly Father has provided the plan and the means for man's salvation. He has given His own Son to die for all the sins of every man. All that is needed is total trust in Christ's death and His shed blood as the payment for that sin. Instead, man rejects this gracious gift as somehow incomplete or unreasonable. "Surely more is needed than this!" they reason. And so they establish their own standard of righteousness.

There is grievous sin involved in this because they are trying to establish their own way to heaven, while rejecting

God's way. In doing this, they have insulted the gift of God. They have said to Him, "I appreciate your effort Lord, but you see, Christ's death on the cross is not enough. And since I am 'as gods, knowing good and evil' (Genesis 3:5), I can make this judgment that you have come up a little short on your plan." What a slap in God's face! What an affront to His love! What arrogance and pride!

This is the very reason Christ called all of mankind's efforts "iniquity;" it exalts the righteousness of man over that of God, "… going about to establish their own righteousness,… (Romans 10:3). These people had arbitrarily chosen their own way over God's. This sin could be greatest of all.

The Scriptures Support It

The clear meaning of Christ's words in contrasting the "few" and the "many" is that many religious people will not make it to heaven. Despite this, many well-meaning Christians cannot imagine that any of the "brethren" may not be brethren after all. The Apostle Peter, speaking for the Twelve, shared this position; "And we believe and are sure that thou art that Christ, the Son of the living God. Jesus answered them, Have not I chosen you twelve, and one of you is a devil?" (John 6:69-70).

The Parable of the virgins in Matthew chapter 25 reveals that 50% are not prepared, the Parable of the Wheat and Tares in Matthew chapter 13 carries the message that the wheat is infiltrated by the tares (weeds) in so pervasive a fashion that one is not able to separate them until the harvest.

The Gospel of John features several stories of those who "believed" in Christ and yet were not saved. In chapter two, "…many believed in his name, … But Jesus did not commit himself unto them, because he knew … what was in man." (vs. 23-25). In chapter eight, many Jews "believed on him" (vs. 30), but this is followed by Christ's stinging indictment of their true condition: "Ye are of your father the devil" (v. 44). This so infuriated them that they took up stones to kill Him (vs. 59). These "believers" were certainly not Christians…

… Nor was Simon Magus. Acts chapter eight records the sad story of this sorcerer and magician who, upon meeting Philip, "believed also." (vs. 13). But when Peter arrived on the scene, he quickly discerned Simon's true state and told him that he had no part in this matter but was still in the bondage of sin. Paul calls this believing "in vain" (1 Corinthians 15:2).

The Scriptures are clear then, that it is possible for a person to make an outward profession of "belief" and faith and never be saved at all! If it can happen in the New Testament, it can certainly happen today.

Church Leaders Agree

Dr. Rod Bell, president of the Fundamental Baptist Fellowship of America, estimates that 50% of church people are without Christ. His estimate concurs with that of Bob Jones, Sr. While in the bookstore of Bob Jones University some time ago, I found a book written by him back in the 1940s in which he also fixed an estimate at 50%.[1] Dr. B. R. Laken estimates that 75% are lost.[2] W.A. Criswell would be surprised to see even 25% of his church members in heaven.[3] Dr. Bob Gray, longtime pastor of the prestigious Trinity Baptist Church of Jacksonville, Florida, once said that probably 75% of those he baptized were not saved.[4] Billy Graham puts the figure at 85% while A.W. Tozer and Southern Baptist consultant Jim Elliff raise it to 90%![5] These are shocking figures to be sure, but they are not surprising. When you weigh the evidence of Christ's own statements and that of the false believers in the Bible, the conclusion is inescapable.

The Barrenness of the Modern Church

Perhaps the most telling evidence of all, however, is the evidence within the church itself.

Its Appeal is Diminishing

Every year in America, almost 4,000 churches close their doors. Currently there are 66,000 closed churches and another 62,000 without pastors. Over eighty percent of churches have plateaued in growth; and of those which do grow, they must credit 80% of that growth to church transfers instead of new conversions. The total number of churches in the U.S. is shrinking yearly from 27 churches for every 10,000 people in 1900 to 12 churches per 10,000 people by 1985. In 1900, a full 66% of the population attended church regularly. It is estimated that by the end of 2000 only 33% will.[6] These depressing figures have prompted pollster George Barna to lament, "The church in America is like the Titanic; it is large, elegant, and sinking fast."[7]

Why this wholesale abandonment of the Church by the populace at large? It is because they see very little difference in the way they live and the way the church lives? … in the victory inside the church and outside it? … in the lives of fellow worldlings compared to those of professing Christians? And is this because, in actuality, the church pews are really filled with an only slightly more sanitized version of the unsaved man on the street?

Its Beliefs are Crumbling

There was a time when the church stood for something, when being "born-again" was more than a presidential interview in a girlie magazine or a description of a revived economy. There was a day in America when it was assumed that "born-again" Christians embraced deep biblical values and beliefs. No more! In recent surveys of so-called "born-again" Christians, it was revealed that many of them have abandoned some long-held convictions. Fifteen percent of them believe that the Bible is not totally accurate, and 29% actually believe that Jesus committed sins. It should be no surprise, then, that 30% deny the resurrection of Christ.

Forty percent believe the Holy Spirit doesn't even exist and 49% agree that Satan is not a living being, merely a symbol of evil.[8]

Gallup reports that 20 percent of born-again Christians believe in reincarnation and 26 percent in astrology. Forty-five percent of those George Barna classifies as born again believe that 'if people are good enough, they can earn a place in heaven' … half of born-again baby boomers believe all religions are 'equally good and true,' almost half have no involvement in a conservative Protestant church, and a quarter believe in communicating with the dead![9] It is hardly a surprise in light of all this that 26 percent of these Christians feel no responsibility whatsoever to witness of their faith. There is little faith to share. Such shocking revelations and the mass drastic departure by "Christians" from a pure faith prompted Paris Reidhead to declare, "The greatest field for evangelism today and in the days ahead is among church members."[10]

Its Godliness is Disappearing

A front-page article in the Washington Times reveals a strange phenomenon in America. The Southern states making up the famous "Bible belt" have one of the highest divorce rates of any region in the country. In fact, the only place with a higher rate is Nevada, home of prostitution and gambling. While Southern Baptists scramble to justify this oddity – with explanations ranging from earlier marriages, the sexual revolution, the pressures of Southern conservatism to marry instead of living together out of wedlock, lower levels of education, and even reduced average incomes, – the question remains. How do you explain the fact that the land of Bible-preaching churches produces twice as many divorces as the Northeast states dominated by liberal theology and modernistic churches?! How does one answer the Barna Research Group's conclusion that overall, "born again Christians are slightly more likely to experience a divorce than non-Christians?"[11] What are we to say to these people? "Become a Christian like us?" Where is the appeal when our marriages are worse off than theirs, when we offer them no answers they don't already possess, when we are really little different than they are? It's true that outwardly we maintain a better way of life. "We don't smoke, we don't chew, and we don't run with them that do," but a "form of godliness without the power thereof" does not win new converts to our faith. The salt loses its savor and the light is hidden under a bushel.

The Apostle Paul warned that such shallowness would characterize the faith in the last days, that many would be known for "Having a form of godliness, but denying the power thereof …" (2 Timothy 3:5). This may be because of the allurement of cheap grace via the attraction of quick outward change without agonizing inner examination. As fool's gold is highly valued by those who've never seen the real thing, and as rhinestones are prized by the uninformed, so a "form of godliness" is the highest evidence of salvation to the ungodly. Perhaps it is the attraction to the "form" which has created so many "Christians" who are barely distinguishable from the non-Christians. Even though these pseudo-Christians may protest it, the fact remains that "They profess that they know God; but in works they deny him, being abominable, and disobedient, and unto every good work reprobate." (Titus 1:16). Luis Palau bemoans the fact that "America is where 80% … claim to be Christians, but few live any differently from pagans or atheists, as though God had no claim on their lives. Their hearts have not been changed."[12] Pollster George Gallup agrees. He finds "very little difference in the behavior of the churched and unchurched on a wide range of items including lying, cheating and stealing."[13]

Hymers asks some hard questions: "Why do [so many] of our people claim to be saved without this having a more positive effect on our crumbling society? Why do so many preachers commit immorality? Why do our churches seem unable to hold on to most of their young people? Why no major revival [in America] for every ninety years?"[10] He believes it is because of a weak theology of salvation and misleading methods of evangelism which have produced a church full of unsaved members. His arguments are weighty and his conclusions demand serious reflection. What has happened to the church?!

Could it be that these churches are losing their effectiveness because many within their ranks are really unbelievers with unchanged hearts? Peter Masters, pastor of the famous Spurgeon Tabernacle in London England observes; "In the history of the Christian Church, the greatest problems have always stemmed from the presence of unsaved people in the church membership."[14]

Perhaps this explains why there is often such dissension and divisiveness in the church today. One national survey indicates that "ninety-nine percent of all pastors reported severe division of one sort or another during their ministries." This same survey reports that eighty-nine percent of independent Baptists have experienced at least "one outright split."[15]

Hymers believes the main responsibility for this disharmony falls directly into the lap of the unregenerate church member. He minces no words. "Most church splits are caused by carnal Christians and lost people pretending to be Christians. Such splits are usually led by lost people (Galatians 5:19-21)."[16]

It is probably that many such lost people find their way into the roles of the church through evangelism methods which are less than thorough.

Misleading Methods

In a country boasting of coast to coast Christianity with thousands of church buildings and millions of members, it is hard to realize the depth of the problem. But once you begin digging, you discover that America's spirituality is a mile wide and only an inch deep. Her shallowness may be traceable to flawed methods at the most crucial point of the conversion experience, the time of the decision itself.

It is at this point that the devil will throw everything

he's got at the seeker to block his decision, to distort his thinking, or to dilute the thoroughness of the process. Much of modern Christendom has played into his hands by adopting ineffective methods of evangelism, many of which seem more geared to instant decisions and full church pews than purity of doctrine and thoroughness of presentation.

Misunderstanding the Means

The reason that so many saved may actually be lost is traceable to a misunderstanding about the means of salvation. Many religious people are misled into believing they are genuine Christians because of some external criteria. This may be the form of their prayer at the time of salvation. It can also include a dependence upon feelings, going forward at a public meeting, or meeting someone's expectations in any regard about the means to salvation.

The Bible warns against dependency upon the wrong things for salvation: "But as many as received him, to them gave he power to become the sons of God, even to them that believe on his name: Which were born, not of blood, nor of the will of the flesh, nor of the will of man, but of God. (John 1:12-13). Salvation comes not from **heredity** ("blood"). You are not a Christian merely because your parents, your nation or your heritage is "Christian."

Nobody becomes a Christian because of **ability** ("the will of the flesh"). Nothing you can do will guarantee you a place in heaven. It is "[n]ot by works of righteousness which we have done, but according to his mercy he saved us, by the washing of regeneration … (Titus 3:5). Despite this scripture, fourteen percent of Americans believe they are Christians because they help other people in some way.

Neither does **philosophy** ("the will of man") save you. It matters not whether it be a formally codified system of religion offered through an organized church or if it is a home-grown philosophy; any belief system apart from God's does not save.

These external approaches to God are man-made, man-centered, man-based, and doomed to failure. Hymers tells of a man whose claim to salvation was a childhood experience which he could not remember although his mother had led him to Christ when he was four years old. He often wondered if he was saved. "Whenever these doubts came to him, he would phone his mother and she would assure him that she remembered his salvation." Hymers comments, "Here is a man whose assurance depended on his mother's memory."[17]

Formula Prayers

In the modern church, as in the Jewish beliefs of Matthew chapter 7, there is an inordinate reliance on the prayer for salvation. Evangelicalism is not excluded from the "every one" of verse 21; "Not every one that saith unto me, Lord, Lord, shall enter into the kingdom of heaven …" The danger then and the danger now is a misguided notion about our prayers. Dr. Dave Breese, in a video produced by the Awana organization[18] offers some examples of prayers used

230

in the evangelism process:

"Will you ask Jesus to come into your heart?" While it is true that when a person becomes a Christian, Christ comes into his life in the form of the Holy Spirit, it is not a means to salvation but a result. There is no scripture which teaches us to "ask Jesus into your heart" as a means to salvation or as a prayer for salvation.

This practice may grow out of a sincere desire to simplify the process for little children. In a recent newsletter from a children's ministry, featuring the testimony of a childhood conversion, reference is made eight times to "inviting Christ into my heart," "asking Jesus into your heart," or "accepting Christ into your heart" with no explanation about the trust or faith that is needed for salvation.

This approach may also be traceable to an erroneous interpretation of the scripture, "He came unto his own, and his own received him not. But as many as received him, to them gave he power to become the sons of God, even to them that believe on his name" (John 1:11-12). Of course, this is a reference to welcoming the presence of Christ in their midst as the Messiah. But becoming the "sons of God" is qualified with the words, "even to them that believe on his name." In other words, salvation comes to those who embraced His deity and messiahship and believed. To believe in this sense means to trust fully and completely. The real essence of salvation is trust! Trusting in Christ's payment of sins and only in Christ's payment. Where is your trust? If it is anywhere but in the shed blood of Christ and His death on the cross, it is misplaced. If it is in your prayer or your act of kneeling in front of the church, it is misplaced. If it is in your baptism or joining the church, it is misplaced. It matters not if you experience a rush of feelings at such times; only trust and faith in Christ's finished work on Calvary is the way to salvation. The Apostle John clarifies this when he says, "even to them that believe on his name." It is believing which saves.

Another common invitation for salvation is "Will you give your heart to God?" We are not saved by giving something to God, but by receiving something from Him.

"Will you make a commitment to Christ?" We are not saved by our commitment to Christ but b y His commitment to us.

"Will you make a decision for Christ?" It is right and good to make a decision but to do what exactly?

"Will you surrender your life to Christ?" may be misleading as well. While "yield," "submit," and "present" are words used in the Bible, they are for believers only.

The common problem with all these invitations is not what they say but what they <u>don't</u> say. The missing element is the heart's trust and faith in Christ's death as the total payment for all my sin. But it is these prayers that I regularly encounter in my counselees as the basis of their salvation. Confused people struggling with doubts and fears for years have prayed these very prayers numerous times and never found peace. I believe it is because a formula prayer is

232

emphasized to the exclusion of heart-felt trust. Could it be a "vain repetition" to lead someone to pray for salvation in a prescribed way rather than teaching them the essence of trust and letting them express it from their heart in their own way?

Would it not be better to emphasize the elements of true salvation and then lead the enquirer to incorporate them into a prayer of his own making? Certainly a heartfelt prayer would go farther than vainly repeating what they think will please the aggressive soul winner. It would also give evidence as to their wholehearted approach to God.

Incomplete Preparation

In order to build the house of trust, the foundation of understanding has to be completed. In her haste to get a seeker to pray a prayer, the church is often guilty of rushing God's preparation process. While it is true that the new birth is an instantaneous act, the pregnancy phase must not be hurried.

King Agrippa said to Paul "... Almost thou persuades me to be a Christian." (Acts 26:28). This means that Agrippa had some knowledge upon which to base that persuasion. In fact, a careful study of this passage reveals that he was an expert in the Jewish religion, was fully aware of Christ's suffering, His death, His resurrection and His mission itself! He even believed the Bible. Paul built upon these things in his appeal to Agrippa to become a Christian.

Although the decision to trust Christ may be quick,

the preparation of heart preceding the decision is not. Salvation is free but not cheap, simple but not easy, and above all, sudden but never fast! Focusing on the persuasion while overlooking the necessary knowledge leading up to it has led to much error.

This is a common danger of the public invitation; it assumes that a person hearing the Gospel for the first time may have all the foundation he needs to make a decision. Worse, it may pressure him to make the decision before he's ready. The problem is compounded by absolute guarantees that "you are now on your way to heaven!" This makes for good statistics on the report of the meeting but for bad complications when years later that "convert" is still struggling with doubts. I believe that many sincere seekers are saved during a public invitation. And this is not to denigrate the practice as much as to emphasize the importance of insuring that each respondent has been adequately prepared and thoroughly counseled before being led to make a decision. Many churches insure this, others don't.

Masters warns of the need of the seeker to have time to come to the place of readiness: "With most believers there was a period of heart searching before they knew that God had washed their sin away, and given them the blessing of a new nature." He writes of God's timing of the actual conversion, "Christ never opens the door of spiritual experience until the Holy Spirit has brought the convicted seeker to sole dependence upon the atoning death of Christ."[19]

"Examine Yourselves"

It is a frightening thing to think that you may not be a Christian after all. You may wonder if I am merely trying to scare you into salvation, but let me assure you that though I would certainly rather scare you into heaven than lull you into hell, my intent is founded upon a biblical admonition. "Examine yourselves, whether ye be in the faith; prove your own selves. Know ye not your own selves ..." (2 Corinthians 13:5). I am trying to motivate you into a careful self-examination, a thorough scrutiny about the state of your eternal soul. I certainly am not the first to do this. Jonathan Edwards, in writing about this verse, said, "... take great care to see that the foundation is right. Those that are in doubt should not give themselves rest till the matter be resolved."[20] Albert Barnes writes, "... all Christians should be often induced to examine the foundation of their hope of eternal salvation."[21] How often? J. Vernon McGee believes "... two or three times a year we should do this. I think every believer ought to do that."[22] Charles Spurgeon agrees. "We must again and again examine ourselves."[23] One reason he gives for this is that you have only this lifetime to make sure of salvation. "Examine yourselves because if ye ake a mistake, ye can never rectify it, except in this world...." He fears that a spirit of presumption or apathy may lead to disaster. "If you do not test yourself, you may sit down and say, 'Oh, I am all right.' Yes, but you may be fostering within your spirit a peace which will end in your final ruin, and you may never open your eyes to your deception till you lift them up in hell."[24]

Re-thinking Our Methods of Evangelism

Any approach to evangelism which fails to fully prepare the seeker's need for adequate understanding is suspect. How many of our "gospel sermons" and "gospel invitations" actually include the gospel? Note the elements of the "Gospel" in Paul's writings: "Moreover, brethren, I declare unto you the gospel which I preached unto you, which also ye have received, and wherein ye stand; By which also ye are saved, if ye keep in memory what I preached unto you, unless ye have believed in vain. For I delivered unto you first of all that which I also received, how that **Christ died for our sins** according to the scriptures; And that **he was buried, and that he rose again the third day** according to the scriptures" (1 Corinthians 15:1-4) [emphasis added]. If the seeker is not given the Gospel or does not understand it, what hope can he have if this is the means "by which ye are saved?"

According to Paul, the Gospel the very basis of salvation, includes the knowledge of Christ's death for our sins, an understanding of His burial, and a comprehension of His resurrection. "That if thou shalt confess with thy mouth the Lord Jesus, and shalt believe in thine heart that God hath raised him from the dead, thou shalt be saved." (Romans 10:9). The Gospel "by which ye are saved" must include all these elements, a full knowledge and understanding of them, along with the trust they invoke in the heart, in order to produce the true salvation. Unfortunately, many religious people who think they are "saved" have never embraced these Gospel truths.

Conclusion

I believe that many religious people will go to hell. I can believe no less after a careful examination of the facts. I no longer assume that a church member is a Christian. Neither do I believe that because a person is a Christian leader or active in Christian service, he is saved.

I am weary of encountering the doubts and fears of an uncertain salvation in the hearts of my counselees. If the church would do a better job of explaining salvation on the front end, she would lighten their load of doubt on the back end.

The Pied Piper of Evangelism

The Town of Hamelin near Hanover City and on the edge of the great Weser River had a serious problem. They were overrun with rats! The city council found a solution. They called on a man renown for working miracles by merely playing tunes on his pipe. He had rid entire communities of moles, toads, snakes, gnats, and even vampire bats. They promised him a handsome fee and sat back to watch him work. No sooner had he begun to play than a mumbling sound soon gave way to a veritable writhing, undulating carpet of dark fur. Thousands and thousands of rats merrily scurried out of their hiding places and cheerfully followed the Piper to the river where they blindly plunged in to their deaths. Upon returning for his fee, the Piper was told by the crafty Mayor that since the rats were dead, there was no more incentive for them to pay.

However, they would give him 5% of what they had promised. Not to be slighted, the Piper reached for his pipe; and with a new tune, he headed once again into the street. No sooner had he begun to play than a mumbling sound followed by a rumbling sound gave way to a laughing, giggling horde of children which grew larger and larger until every child in the village was following the Piper out of town. He made a turn at the river, however, and headed for the sheer face of a mountain. As he approached, it opened up and he led all the children in. the mountain closed on them and they were never seen again. What began as a desire to rid the earth of rats, but he mere change of tune, ended in the loss of an entire generation of the village children.

I wonder if this is not a picture of the problem before us. Is it possible tha the Evangelistic Piper who intended to rid the world of sin has changed his tune so drastically that he is leading a generation blindly toward the face of the mountain? Has what began as a desire to rid the earth of sin led to the loss of the very sinners it originally set out to save? Has the plan of salvation been so simplified and the presentation of the Gospel so abbreviated that the change of tune is leading the laughing, giggling, hordes into error and even damnation?

What is to be done? The solution is not to kill the Piper. The rats would have no opposition. No good would come from the elimination of evangelism outright, except the proliferation of sin.

Neither is the solution to amplify the corrupting tune

over loudspeakers so it can be heard in outlying villages and lands. Using modern technology to spread an incomplete gospel is not the answer either.

Nor is the answer a mere alteration of the tone being piped. It's not enough to merely correct the pitch of a deceptive tune. A slight alteration to a flawed plan of evangelism is no more effective than a slight course changed by the Titanic when the iceberg was spotted.

What is needed is to change the tune! A re-examination of our entire approach to evangelism is necessary. From child evangelism to weekly church visitation, from street witnessing to church altar counseling – a change is needed.

If you're a soul winner, maybe you need to examine your techniques and your approach to evangelism. As one man observed, "It takes four hours for a baby giraffe to be born and give minutes for a baby Christian!" Maybe we need to rethink this. Are you thoroughly presenting the Gospel?

If you're the Shepherd of a flock, maybe you need to "know your sheep and call them by name." Each individual sheep may need examination to be sure that he is not really a goat or worse yet, a wolf in sheep's clothing. Hymers recommends that each pastor personally lead each inquirer to Christ. That would certainly provide a greater certainty of their spiritual state.

Just as important is a rethinking of your own position in Christ. If you're one of the "good" people who are relying on your good works, you need to "examine yourself, whether ye be in the faith."

It's not too late to change the tune. The alternative is unthinkable.

Footnotes:

1 Jones Sr., Dr. Bob, *What is a Christian*, BJU Press.
2 Branson, Roy, *Dear Abner, I Love You. Joab*, Landmark Publishing, Bristol, Tenn., 1992, p. 298.
3 Hymers, R.L., and Cagan, Christopher, *Preaching to a Dying Nation*, F.B.T. Publishers, 1999, p. VIII.
4 *The Gist*, Spring Isue, 1997, p. 5.
5 Hymers Cagan, p. VIII.
6 Kroll, Woodrow, *The Vanishing Ministry*, Kregen Publishers, 1991, pp. 31-33.
7 Hymers & Cagan, p. VIII.
8 *Baptist Bible Tribune*, April 15, 1996, p. 28.
9 Reidhead, Paris, *Getting Evangelicals Saved*, Bethany House Publishing, 1989, p. 47.
10 Hymers & Cagan, Today's Apostasy: *How Decisionism is Destroying Our Churches,* Hearthstone Pub., 1999, p. 5
11 *Washington Times*, July 24, 2000.
12 Palau, Luis, *The Only Hope for America*, Crossway Books, 1996, p. 10.
13 *Los Angeles Herald Examiner*, July 14, 1984, p. 24.
14 Masters, Peter, *Seven Certain Signs of True Conversion*, London: Sword & Trowel, 1976, p. 20.
15 *Los Angeles Times*, January 6, 1996, p. B-11.
16 *Today's Apostasy*, p. 76.
17 Ibid., p. 37.
18 Breese, David, video entitled Blessed Calvary.
19 Masters, Peter, Sword Trowel, 2000, no. 1. P. 20.
20 Edwards, Jonathan, *The Works of Jonathan Edwards*, Volume Two, Banner of Truth, 1992, p. 174.
21 Barnes, Albert, *Notes on the New Testament, 1 Corinthians*, Baker, 1983, p. 268.
22 McGee, J. Vernon, *Through the Bible*, Nelson Publishers, 1983, Vol. 5, p. 145.

23 Spurgeon, C.H., *Metropolitan Tabernacle Pulpit*, Vol. 30, Pilgrim Pub., 1973, p. 371.

24 Ibid., p. 371.

Editor's Note: I am indebted to Drs. Hymers and Cagan for their thorough research on effective evangelism. Many references listed here are gleaned from their labor.

Getting to Know Us
L.E.A.D. Ministries
Crisis Counseling for Those in Ministry

Getting to Know Us

Dr. Jim Binney has been a pastor, teacher, youth pastor, church planter, and executive administrator. He served as a pastor for 16 years in three churches and more recently served as Interim Pastor for Calvary Baptist Church in Simpsonville, SC and Faith Baptist Church in Taylors, SC. He knows well both the blessings and rigors of the ministry. He founded L.E.A.D. Ministries in 1989 when he came to Moorehead Manor with his wife Sandra. L.E.A.D.'s primary focus is ministering to Christian leaders who are now more than ever under the attack of Satan.

He has drawn upon the strength and grace of God to help these leaders in need; and he and his wife have ministered to hundreds of Christian leaders who have come for help in their week-long program of counseling and renewal. Although the location has moved from Ohio to

South Carolina, the ministry has stayed focused on helping those who are in the forefront of the battle, those in full-time Christian service.

Our Mission

The primary goal of L.E.A.D. Ministries is to encourage pastors, deacons and other leaders in ministry, through biblical counseling.

Hundreds of leaders and their wives have come for counseling since 1989. After spending a week of counseling, many have seen broken marriages restored, some have received a renewed vision for their ministry, others have experienced victory over personal struggles, but all have clearly seen the value of Christ's counsel about taking time out from the ministry to gain a fresh perspective: "And he said unto them, Come ye yourselves apart into a desert place, and rest a while: for there were many coming and going, and they had no leisure so much as to eat" (Mark 6:31).

Dr. Binney's philosophy behind personal counseling is that the Bible is sufficient to address every need. The Word of God is central in restoring hope to the discouraged, in revealing misconceptions about God's expectations and in renewing relationships. That philosophy permeates every other facet of the ministry.

Testimonies

"The ONLY reason I am still in the ministry today is because you skillfully and lovingly applied the Word of God to my life and situation. Your book 'The Ministry of Marriage' has made me the Christian husband I always wanted to be - **but didn't know how to be**! My wife and I are excited about the possibility of working on our marriage at one of your week-long sesions. You mean so much to me - I will spend the rest of my ministry making you glad that you invested your ministry in my life !!!"

Pastor, Florida

"Thank you for the renewed hope you have given us. We look forward to getting back in the ministry with His strength and His wisdom."

Pastor and Wife, Michigan

"Your counseling is accurate, penetrating and healing. It is a biblical 'bomb' and balm. You and Sandra are hand and glove. Thank you for holding us."

Assistant Pastor, Illinois

"You have made me feel so safe and accepted. It is significant to me that someone we've only just met could show such love and compassion. Thank you for never judging, even when the deepest secrets came out."

Pastor and Wife, California

Other Books by the Author

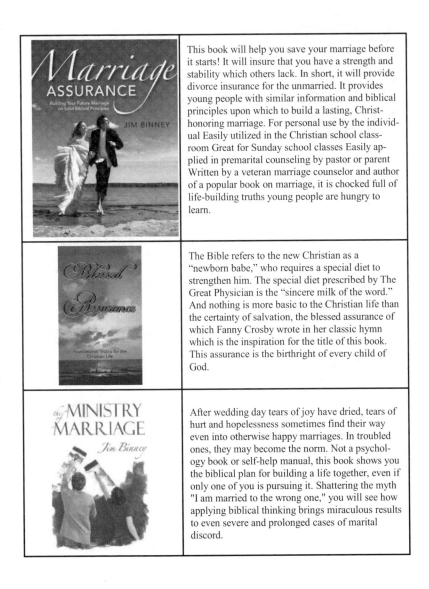

Marriage ASSURANCE — Building Your Future Marriage on Solid Biblical Principles — JIM BINNEY	This book will help you save your marriage before it starts! It will insure that you have a strength and stability which others lack. In short, it will provide divorce insurance for the unmarried. It provides young people with similar information and biblical principles upon which to build a lasting, Christ-honoring marriage. For personal use by the individual Easily utilized in the Christian school classroom Great for Sunday school classes Easily applied in premarital counseling by pastor or parent Written by a veteran marriage counselor and author of a popular book on marriage, it is chocked full of life-building truths young people are hungry to learn.
Blessed Assurance — Foundational Truths for the Christian Life	The Bible refers to the new Christian as a "newborn babe," who requires a special diet to strengthen him. The special diet prescribed by The Great Physician is the "sincere milk of the word." And nothing is more basic to the Christian life than the certainty of salvation, the blessed assurance of which Fanny Crosby wrote in her classic hymn which is the inspiration for the title of this book. This assurance is the birthright of every child of God.
the MINISTRY MARRIAGE — Jim Binney	After wedding day tears of joy have dried, tears of hurt and hopelessness sometimes find their way even into otherwise happy marriages. In troubled ones, they may become the norm. Not a psychology book or self-help manual, this book shows you the biblical plan for building a life together, even if only one of you is pursuing it. Shattering the myth "I am married to the wrong one," you will see how applying biblical thinking brings miraculous results to even severe and prolonged cases of marital discord.

	With surgical precision, a biblical counselor exposes the wound of sexual immorality; he then pours in the soothing Balm of Gilead to bring healing.
	Basic foundational principles of biblical counseling are featured in a live, 10-session seminar presentation by Dr. Binney. Taught to pastors and laymen alike in church, seminar and Bible college settings, this album provides practical biblical tools for the counselor or those seeking personal growth.
	A pre-marital seminar as taught by Dr. Jim Binney to the students at Bob Jones University, this series helps to prepare a couple for a lasting, Christ-centered marriage. Building on a firm foundation of biblical precepts, you will be taught life-giving principles for developing a healthy marriage.

For more information on our products, contact us or visit our website.

L.E.A.D. Ministries
Email: counselor@leadministries.net
Website: www.leadministries.net